ANSWERS TO LIFE'S
DIFFICULT QUESTIONS

ANSWERS
TO LIFE'S DIFFICULT
QUESTIONS

RICK WARREN

The Encouraging Word

Phone: 949/888-2500
Fax: 949/888-2600
Internet: www.pastors.net

Other Books By Rick Warren

The Purpose Driven Church
Personal Bible Study Methods
The Power to Change Your Life

7 8 9 10 11   Printing/Year   94 93 92 91 99

Except where otherwise indicated, Scripture quotations in this book are taken from the *Holy Bible, New International Version,* © 1973, 1978, 1984, International Bible Society. Used by permission of Zondervan Bible Publishers. Other Bible quotations are from the *King James Version* (Kjv) and *The New Testament in Modern English* (PII), Revised Edition, © J.B. Phillips, 1958, 1960, 1972, permission of Macmillan Publishing Co. and Collins Publishers.

Recommended Dewey Decimal Classification: 248.8
Suggested Subject Heading: PERSONAL CHRISTIANITY

Library of Congress Catalog Card Number: 85-50317
ISBN: 0-9660895-2-9

The Encouraging Word, Inc.
www.rickwarren.com

CONTENTS

I dedicate this book to my flock, the
members of Saddleback Valley Community Church.
They have an insatiable hunger for practical teaching
from God's Word, listen intently, and seek to
apply the truth to their lives. I am grateful
to be their pastor.

Many books today deal with the theme of self-improvement. Everyone wants to change for the better. Americans will spend millions of dollars this year in their search for practical solutions to their problems. Some will move from one fad to another, looking for advice on how to live and for answers to perplexing questions.

Unfortunately, much of the advice being dispensed these days through television, radio, and print is highly unreliable. It is based on popular opinion and current thinking. Today's "pop psychology" will be discarded next year for a new approach or therapy.

Jesus said, "You shall know the truth, and the truth shall set you free!" Lasting freedom from personal hang-ups comes from building our lives on the truth. Only the Bible can be totally depended on to provide truthful insights into the causes and cures for our personal problems. God's Word has stood the test of time. It is just as relevant and applicable today as it was thousands of years ago. It contains the answers to life's most difficult questions.

However, it is not enough to simply say, "The Bible is the answer." It is important for Christians to show *how* the Bible answers life's questions. In this book I've tried to identify practical steps and specific actions you can take, based on God's Word, which will help you cope with the common problems we all face. D.L. Moody once said, "The Bible was not given to increase our knowledge, but to change our lives."

When Jesus taught, His intention was that those who listened would "go and do likewise." He aimed for specific actions and commitments. In each of these twelve studies you'll discover simple ways to apply God's truth to your personal life, your family, and your job. The way to get the most out of this book is to act on it!

Why are there so many biographical stories in the Bible? The Apostle Paul said, "Everything that was written in the past was written to teach us, so that through endurance and encouragement of the Scriptures, we might have hope" (Rom. 15:4). God gave us these examples from people's lives for two reasons.

First, they are given to teach us. It is always wise to learn from our own experiences, but it is even wiser to learn from the experiences of others. It is usually less painful too! By applying the principles illustrated in the lives of Bible characters, we can avoid making some of the same costly mistakes they made.

Second, God gave us these stories to encourage us. We are encouraged by the fact that God chooses to use ordinary people to accomplish His plans—in spite of their weaknesses and failures and sometimes mixed motives. That gives us hope that God can work in our lives too!

It is my prayer that these studies of Bible characters will produce two results in your life: that you will learn God's principles for successful living, and that you will believe God can use you in a significant way.

CHAPTER ONE

How Can I Cope with Stress?

Jesus Christ was constantly under pressure. There were grueling demands on His time; He rarely had any personal privacy; He was constantly interrupted; people repeatedly misunderstood Him, criticized Him, and ridiculed Him. He had enormous stress which would have caused any of us to cave in.

But as we look at the life of Christ we quickly discover that He remained at peace under pressure. He was never in a hurry. He was always at ease. He had a calmness about His life that enabled Him to handle enormous amounts of stress. How did He do this so successfully? He based His life on sound principles of stress management. If we understand and apply these principles in our lives, we'll experience less pressure and more peace of mind.

IDENTIFICATION: KNOW WHO YOU ARE

Jesus said, "I am the Light of the world. Whoever follows Me will never walk in darkness, but will have the light of the world. Whoever follows Me will never walk in darkness, but will have the light of life" (John 8:12). "I am the Door" (10:9, KJV); "I am the Way and the Truth and the Life" (14:6); "I am the Good Shepherd" (10:11); "I am God's Son" (10:36). Christ knew who He was!

The first principle for handling stress in your life is this: *Know who you are.* It is the principle of identification. Jesus said, "I know who I am. I testify to Myself." This is critically important in stress management because if you don't know who you are, somebody else may try to tell you who *he* thinks you are. If you don't know who you are, you will let other people manipulate you and pressure you into being somebody you aren't.

A lot of stress in life results from our wearing masks, being unreal with others, living double lives, or trying to be somebody we're not. Insecurity always produces pressure in our lives, and when we're insecure we feel pressured to perform and conform. We set unrealistic standards for our lives, and even though we work, work, work, we can't meet those unrealistic standards. Tension and pressure naturally occur as a result.

The first way to balance stress in my life is to get an internal balance of who I am. And I know *who* I am by knowing *whose* I am. I am a child of God. I was put on earth not by accident but for a purpose. I am deeply loved by God. I am accepted by Him. He has a plan for my life, and because He put me here I am significant.

And because He put *you* here, *you* are significant. To handle stress you must know who you are. Until you handle this issue, you'll be pressured by insecurity.

DEDICATION: KNOW WHOM YOU'RE TRYING TO PLEASE

The second principle of stress management in the life of Christ is found in John 5:30: "By Myself I can do nothing; I judge only as I hear, and My judgment is just, for I seek not to please Myself, but Him who sent Me."

The principle is this: *Know whom you're trying to please.* You know you can't please everybody, because just about the time you get one group pleased, another group gets mad at you. Even God doesn't please everybody, so it's foolish to try to do something that even God doesn't do!

Jesus knew whom He was trying to please; it was a settled issue with Him: "I'm going to please God the Father." And the Father replied, "This is My beloved Son, in whom I am well pleased" (Matt. 3:17, KJV).

When you don't know whom you're trying to please, you cave in to three things: *criticism* (because you are concerned about what others will think about you), *competition* (because you worry about whether somebody else is getting ahead of you), and *conflict* (because you're threatened when anyone disagrees with you).

If I seek first the kingdom of God and His righteousness, then all the other necessary things of life will be added unto me (Matt. 6:33). This means that if I focus on pleasing God, it will simplify my life. I will always be doing the right thing, the thing that pleases God, regardless of what anybody else thinks.

We love to blame our stress on other people: "You *made* me . . . I *have* to . . . I've *got* to." Actually there are few things in life (outside of our employment) that we *must* do. When we say, "I have to, I must, I've got to," we are actually saying, "I choose to, because I don't want to pay the consequences.'' Hardly anybody *makes* us do anything, so usually we can't blame other people for our stress. When we get under pressure we are *choosing* to allow other people to put us under pressure. We are not victims unless we *allow* ourselves to be pressured by other people's demands.

ORGANIZATION: KNOW WHAT YOU'RE TRYING TO ACCOMPLISH

Here is Christ's third principle for dealing with stress: "Even if I testify on My own behalf, My testimony is valid, for I know where I came from and where I am going" (John 8:14). The principle is this: *Know what you want to accomplish.* Christ said, "I know where I came from and I know where I'm going." Unless you plan your life, and set priorities, you'll be pressured by what other people think is important.

Every day you either live by priorities or you live by pressures. There is no other option. You either decide what is important in your life or else you let other people tell you what is most important in your life. You set priorities or you live by pressures.

It's so easy to operate under the tyranny of the urgent, to come to the end of your day and think, "Have I really accomplished anything? I used a lot of energy and did a lot of things, but did I accomplish anything important?" Busyness is not necessarily productivity. You may be spinning in circles without accomplishing anything.

Preparation causes you to be at ease. To put it another way, "Preparation prevents pressure but procrastination produces it." Good organization and good preparation reduce stress because you know who you are, whom you're trying to please, and what you want to accomplish. Having clear goals greatly simplifies life. Spend a few minutes each day in prayer talking with God. Look at your schedule for the day and decide, "Is this really the way I want to spend a day of my life? Am I willing to exchange twenty-four hours of my life for these activities?"

CONCENTRATION: FOCUS ON ONE THING AT A TIME

At least some people tried to get Jesus detoured from His planned schedule. They tried to distract Him from His goal in life. At daybreak Jesus went out to a solitary place to be alone. But the people went looking for Him even there, and when they found Him "they tried to keep Him from leaving them" (Luke 4:42). He was going to leave but they tried to make Him stay.

Here is how Jesus responded: "I must preach the Good News of the kingdom of God to the other towns also, because that is why I was sent" (v. 43). He refused to be distracted by less important matters.

Principle number four for stress management is this: *Focus on one thing at a time.* It is the principle of concentration. Jesus was a master at this. It seemed that everybody tried to interrupt Him; everyone had a Plan B for Him. But Jesus responded, "Sorry, I must keep on moving toward My goal." He kept right on doing what He knew God had told Him to do: preach about the kingdom of God. He was determined. He was persistent. He concentrated His efforts.

When I've got thirty things to do on my desk, I clear

my desk and work on one thing. When I finish that I pick up something else. You can't catch two jackrabbits at once. You've got to focus on one. When we diffuse our efforts, we are ineffective. When we concentrate our efforts, we are more effective. Light diffused produces a hazy glow, but light concentrated produces fire. Use a magnifying glass to concentrate light on a dry leaf, and that leaf will catch fire. Light without a magnifying glass will have no effect, but the glass concentrates it to produce power. Jesus Christ did not let interruptions prevent Him from concentrating on His goal; He did not let others make Him tense or stressed or irritated.

DELEGATION: DON'T DO IT ALL YOURSELF

One day "Jesus went up into the hills and called to Him those He wanted, and they came to Him" (Mark 3:13). He appointed twelve men whom He designated as apostles, so they might be with Him and He could send them out to preach. In other words, He delegated His authority. This is the fifth principle: *Don't try to do it all yourself.* Use the principle of delegation.

Do you know why we get uptight and tense? Because we think everything depends on us. Here I am, Atlas, holding up the cares of the world—they're all on my shoulders. If I happen to let go, the world will fall apart. But when I really do let go, the world doesn't fall apart! Jesus enlisted and trained twelve disciples so that they could share the load. He delegated His work. He got other people involved.

Why don't we delegate? Why don't we get other people involved? Why do we try to do it all ourselves?

For two reasons. The first reason is *perfectionism*. We think, "If I want a job well done, I'll do it myself." That's a nice idea, but often it doesn't work well because there are just too many things to be done. We simply don't have time to do everything. It's really an egotistical attitude that says, "Nobody, but nobody, can do it like I can."

Do you think Jesus would have done a better job than these disciples? Of course He would have. But He let them do the work even though He would have done it better. We need to let other people make some of the mistakes. Don't rob others of an education!

The other reason we don't delegate is because of personal *insecurity*. "What if I turn over this responsibility to someone and he does a better job at it?" That thought is kind of threatening to us. But you won't be threatened by that possibility if you know who you are, whom you're trying to please, what you want to accomplish, and what one thing you want to focus on. In order to be effective you *must* get other people involved, because you can't focus on more than one thing at a time and do it effectively.

MEDITATION: MAKE A HABIT OF PERSONAL PRAYER

Jesus often got up "very early in the morning, while it was still dark . . . and went off to a solitary place" to pray (Mark 1:35). The sixth principle of stress management is to *make a habit of personal prayer*. This is the principle of meditation. Prayer is a gigantic stress-reliever. It is a God-given tool for letting off your anxieties. No matter how busy Jesus got, He made it a practice to spend time alone with God. If *Jesus* made time for prayer when He was busy, how much more do you and I need prayer! A quiet time, getting alone with God, can be a decompression chamber for life's stresses. We talk with God in prayer, tell Him what's on our minds, and let Him talk to us as we read the Bible. Then we look at our schedules, evaluate our priorities, and wait for instructions. (In my book *Personal Bible Study Methods [Encouraging Word]* there is a detailed explanation of how to develop and continue the habit of a daily devotional time with God.)

Many of our problems come from our inability to sit still. We just don't know how to be quiet. Most of us cannot sit in a car for five minutes without turning the radio on.

If you walk into your house and find that you're all alone, what's the first thing you do? (Probably turn on the TV.) Silence makes us uncomfortable. But God says, "Be still and know that I am God" (Ps. 46:10). One reason many people don't know God personally is that they can't be still. They're too busy to be quiet and think.

Someone said, "It seems to be an ironic habit of man that when he loses his way he doubles his speed" —like an Air Force pilot in World War II who flew out over the Pacific. When he radioed in, the controller asked, "Where are you?"

The pilot replied, "I don't know, but I'm making record time!" A lot of people are like that: they are speeding through life but they don't know where they are headed. We need to start our morning with prayer, as Jesus did, and then periodically through the day stop and pray again, to recharge our spiritual batteries.

RECREATION: TAKE TIME OFF TO ENJOY LIFE

Once Jesus' twelve men gathered around Him and reported all that they had done and taught. Because so many people were coming and going they hadn't even been able to eat. So Jesus said to them, "Come with Me by yourselves to a quiet place and get some rest" (Mark 6:31). Principle number seven for stress management is to *take time off to enjoy life*. It's the principle of relaxation and recreation. Jesus looked at these men who had been working hard without relief and said, "You deserve a break today. Let's get some rest. Let's take some time off." So they got in a boat, rowed to the other side of the lake, and went out to the desert to rest.

One reason why Jesus could handle stress is that He knew when to relax. He frequently went either to the mountains or the desert just to unwind.

Rest and recreation in life are not optional. In fact, rest is so important that God included it in the Ten Commandments. The Sabbath was made for man because God knows that our physical, emotional, and spiritual constitutions demand periodic breaks. Jesus survived stress because He enjoyed life. One of my favorite verses, Matthew 11:19 in the Phillips paraphrase, says that Jesus came "enjoying life." Paul wrote that God has provided everything richly for our enjoyment (1 Tim. 6:17). Balance in life is a key to stress management.

TRANSFORMATION: GIVE YOUR STRESS TO CHRIST

The eighth principle of stress management is one that Jesus didn't need because He is the Son of God, but we need it because we're merely human. Jesus says, "Come to Me, all you who are weary and burdened, and I will give you rest. Take My yoke upon you and learn from Me, for I am gentle and humble in heart, and you will find rest for your souls. For My yoke is easy and My burden is light" (Matt. 11:28-30). So this final principle of stress management is: *Give your stress to Christ.* You will never enjoy complete peace of mind until you have a relationship with the Prince of Peace.

Christ did *not* say, "Come to Me and I will give you more guilt, more burdens, more stress, and more worries"—even though that's what a lot of people seem to teach! Some churches tend to create pressure rather than relieve it. But Jesus said, "I want to give you *rest.* I am the Stress-Reliever. When you get in harmony with Me, I will give you inner strength." Christ can transform your lifestyle from stressful to satisfied. The greatest source of stress comes from trying to live our lives apart from the One who made us, trying to go our own ways, and be our own gods.

What do you need? If you've never committed your life to Christ, you need a transformation. Give your life with all its stresses to Him and say, "Lord, please give me a new life. Replace the pressure I feel with the peace You offer. Help me follow Your principles of stress management."

CHAPTER TWO

How Can I Rebound from Failure?

A failure can become a stepping-stone to success. An incident from Peter's life (Luke 5:1-11) illustrates this wonderful truth. Peter and his friends had been out fishing all night, but they had caught nothing. This was probably unusual, since Peter was a professional fisherman. He definitely was not a novice. Probably he had the best nets, a good boat, and he knew exactly where to catch the most fish. He had worked all night, as his income depended on a good catch. But still Peter came up short. Even the superstars strike out sometimes.

Next day the disciples were washing their nets on the seashore, feeling very tired and discouraged. At that moment Jesus came along and said, "Peter, I'd like to use your boat as a platform to speak from." So Peter let Jesus get into his boat and launched out a little way from the shore. There Jesus could speak from the boat to the crowd standing on the shore.

After finishing His message Jesus said to the disciples,

"Now let's go fishing. Launch out into the deep water," He said, "and let down the nets for a catch." But Peter replied, "Master, we've worked hard all night and haven't caught anything—yet if You say so, I'll let down the nets." When the disciples obeyed, they caught such a large number of fish that their nets began to break.

WHEN OUR BEST IS NOT ENOUGH

What does this story teach us about failure? Jesus never did a miracle without a purpose. He always used His miracles to illustrate principles. This incident teaches us what to do when our best is not good enough.

Sometimes you give it your best shot but you still come up ten feet short. You study diligently for a test but only get a "C." You work hard to make your marriage better but still don't see any progress. Life can be tough at times and it's tempting to give up. You feel like saying, "What's the use? I just set myself up for more failure. Can anything make a difference?"

The interesting part of this story is the comparison between the two catches. The disciples had worked all night and had caught nothing, but later they went out for ten minutes and caught more than ever before. It was the same lake, the same boat, the same nets, and the same people fishing. So what made the difference?

There are actually three differences between the two fishing expeditions, and these differences give us principles to follow when our best attempts end in failure. I believe any person who applies these principles will be a genuine success in life. God intended them to be easy to understand, so that everybody could get in on the benefit. But first you must realize God is interested in your success; He's not interested in seeing you Fail. Suppose my daughter Amy said to me one day, "Daddy, I'm a total failure in life. Everything I touch falls apart. My problems are insurmountable. I can never do anything right. I'm a total failure and I'll never change." Would I reply, "Oh, I'm so happy you told me that! That makes me feel so good inside"? No, of course not. As a father I want my children to be successful, to be the best they can be. Likewise your Heavenly Father wants you to be successful in life too—in your personal life, your family, your spiritual growth, and in all your relationships.

APPROPRIATE GOD'S PRESENCE IN YOUR LIFE
The first principle of success is found in Luke 5:3: *Jesus was in the boat with the disciples.* Christ's presence made a big difference! This time the disciples weren't fishing by themselves; God was with them. The first principle for successful living is this: *You must appropriate God's presence in your life.* In other words, you've got to get Jesus in your boat. That's the starting point. Nothing has greater influence on your personal success than whether or not you are living with Christ in your life. Now in Peter's life his boat represented his livelihood. When you're a fisherman, that boat is your business! It's significant that Peter made his boat available for Jesus to use. Christ used Peter's business as a platform for ministry.

Does God have access to your job? Is your business available for Him to use at any time? Is He able to minister to people through your job? Too often we try to separate the secular and the spiritual. We have our Christian life nicely partitioned off from our career. But this prevents God from blessing your business or job. God will bless anything you give Him. If you give Him all your life, He'll bless all of it. But if you give Him just a part of it, He'll bless just that one part.

A friend told me that as president of his corporation he invites God to every board meeting. He reports that as a result they make fewer mistakes, and have more peace of mind about difficult decisions.

There's something about having Jesus in your boat that eliminates the fear of failure and reduces your worries about the results. When Peter made Christ his fishing partner, the results were incredible: he caught more fish than he had ever caught on his own. Don't miss the sequence, though. First Peter used his boat *for Christ's purposes.* Jesus took the boat and preached from it to reach people. Then, after Christ had used the boat for His own purposes, God took care of Peter's needs.

God promises us that if we "Seek . . . first the king-dom of God and His righteousness . . . all these [other] things shall be added" unto us (Matt. 6:33, KJV). Does that mean if I give my whole life to Christ, putting Him first in every area, then will He bless it all? Yes, that is God's promise to you.

COOPERATE WITH GOD'S PLAN

The second principle is found in Luke 5:4: The second time the disciples went fishing, they fished under the direction of Christ, obediently following His instructions. We must not only appropriate God's presence in our lives, but we must *cooperate with God's presence in our lives.* Jesus told the disciples where to fish, when to fish, and how to fish. *When God is guiding your life, you cannot fail.* As Ethel Waters says, "God doesn't sponsor flops."

Peter's reaction to Christ's guidance was beautiful. First, he didn't argue. He didn't say, "Wait a minute, Jesus. Who are You to tell me how to fish? Don't You know I'm Simon Peter? I'm the premier professional fisherman on this lake. I own the record. Who are You to tell me how to fish?" He didn't ask, "Lord, are You sure?" Also he didn't hesitate and he didn't ask any questions. He might have been thinking that if he didn't catch anything at night he certainly was not going to catch anything in the middle of the day when the sun was glaring down on the water. From a human standpoint it was bad timing—it seemed ridiculous. But Peter didn't ask any questions; he just obeyed.

Also, he didn't listen to his feelings. I'm sure he was dog-tired from working all night but he didn't ask, "What's the use? Why should I keep on going?" Peter's attitude was perfect. He was eager to cooperate with God's plan.

Why do you think Jesus said to Peter, "Launch out into the deep?" I think it was because it's in the deep water that the big fish are located. You only catch minnows in shallow water. Most people live in the shallow waters of life. They simply exist on a superficial level. There's little depth to their lives because they're content to just play around the edge, never getting out into deeper water. Why? Because it's safer in shallow water. They think, "If I get out into the deep water there might be some waves. They might rock my boat, and it might overturn. So I'll just stay back here where it's safe and comfortable and piddle around.''

When God works in your life it always involves risks, because God wants you to live by faith. Many Christians barely get their feet wet because they're afraid of getting in over their heads. They think, "If I really get serious about my commitment to the Lord, He may make me a fanatic. I may become a religious nut. What will my friends think?" So they're content to live in the shallows of life—and they miss out on so much.

God's plan for your life is a good plan, one that will work for your benefit. God says, "Let Me get into your boat. Let My presence be with you wherever you go—in your business, in your family, in your marriage, in every area. Let Me direct you, and cooperate with My plan."

EXPECT GOD TO ACT

The third principle is found in verse 5: "*Because You say so.*" To rebound from failure you must *anticipate God's promises in your life.* In the second fishing attempt the disciples were acting on the basis of God's promise to them. They went fishing again because they believed God would provide the fish. Now Jesus didn't specifically say, "Peter, if you go fishing with Me, I promise you'll make a big catch." He didn't need to say that because Peter realized that when Christ told him to go fishing, and also got into the boat, and also told him exactly where to put down the net, it wasn't going to come up empty! Peter expected God to act. He expected God would keep His promise. Peter wasn't merely depending on his own fishing ability, so he wasn't afraid of failure. He anticipated the promises of God.

When you get God's presence in your boat, and when you get God's plan in your head, and when you get God's promises in your heart, you cannot fail. Start expecting some wonderful results.

IT CAN WORK IN YOUR LIFE

Maybe you're saying, "That sounds great, but you don't know my circumstances. Right now I'm defeated by the problems I'm experiencing. I'm having some hard times." If you are defeated by your circumstances, let me suggest an antidote for you. Begin reading your Bible to find a specific promise from God, and then start claiming it. Start expecting God to act, and you will find that God's promise will inject new hope into a hopeless situation. Real success often begins at the point of failure.

I know a married couple who've had a severely damaged relationship, one that looked irreparable. But they sensed God saying to them, "I want you to stay together. Don't give up."

Without any outward evidence they took the attitude of Peter: "Lord, we've worked on this marriage a long time, without improvement, but because You say so, we'll keep at it." Today they have a fulfilling marriage and a dynamic ministry together.

Look at the results (v. 6): the disciples caught such a large number of fish that their nets began to break. God blessed them with more than they could handle. That is always the case when you appropriate God's presence, cooperate with God's plan, and anticipate God's promises—you'll be blessed with more than you can handle. In fact, verse 7 points out that the disciples had to share the results with those in another boat in order to keep from sinking! That's a great way to live!

The point is this: God not only wants to bless your life. He wants to bless you so much that you have to share your blessing with others in order to keep yourself from sinking. He not only wants to bless *you*, but He wants to bless *other people through you*—people whose nets are empty. God blessed them with more than they could use for themselves.

The miracle so astounded Peter that he cried out, "Lord, I don't deserve this! I'm a sinner. This is too good for me." The incident became a turning point in Peter's life and in the lives of the other disciples.

Jesus then said to Peter, "Don't be afraid; from now on you will catch men" (v. 10). So the disciples beached their boats and left everything to follow Jesus.

Think about that—when the fishing party got to land, they left the greatest catch they had ever experienced sitting right there on the shore and went after Jesus! They realized that if Jesus could perform a miracle like that, He could do anything He wanted to. They knew as long as they followed Him, their needs would be more than satisfied. Christ would take care of them no matter what happened. They wanted a relationship with Him that was more than a one-time miracle. Then Christ invited them to become part of the greatest task in the world: "I'm going to make you fishers of men. You're going to share My Good News with other people."

TRY IT AGAIN WITH CHRIST

How does this story relate to your life? Maybe you feel like the disciples before Christ came along: "I've worked all night and come up with an empty net." Does that describe your attitude toward your marriage, your job, or toward another personal problem? You feel that you haven't made any progress so you've said to yourself, "What's the use? Why keep on trying? Why put forth the effort?" Maybe you've become a little cynical about life.

Peter didn't get cynical. He didn't say, "Lord, I've worked ten hours and didn't catch anything. That must mean there are no more fish in this lake." He knew that the fish were there, but that he just hadn't caught them yet.

Just because you haven't solved your problem doesn't mean there isn't a solution. Through failure we often learn the lessons that help us succeed. God's message to you is this: *Don't give up.* Try again, but this time do it with Jesus in your boat. He will make all the difference.

CHAPTER
THREE

How Can I Defeat Depression?

Depression is one of the great problems in the world today. It has been called the common cold of emotional illnesses. Everybody gets depressed at times, but some people are depressed nearly all the time. Even great saints get depressed, and Elijah was just such an example.

Elijah was a tremendous spokesman for God. For three years he had been God's mouthpiece to the nation of Israel. All kinds of miracles had taken place, and there was a spiritual awakening in his nation which had been going after pagan idols.

But one person who did not like Elijah was Jezebel, the Queen of Israel. A very wicked woman, Jezebel hated Elijah, partly because he had so much influence. After one particularly great miracle performed by Elijah, Jezebel's husband, King Ahab, told Jezebel everything that Elijah had done. This made her so angry that she sent a messenger to Elijah saying, "May the gods deal with me, be it ever so severely, if by this time tomorrow I do not make your life like that of one of them" (1 Kings 19:2). She was saying, "If I don't kill you within twenty-four hours, I'll be ready to kill myself."

Here's the Elijah who had been fearless for three years, and now, when one woman threatens his life, he becomes frightened, runs out to the desert, and gets depressed (vv. 3-5). He comes to a broom tree, sits down under it, and prays that he might die. "I have had enough, Lord. Take my life. I am no better than my ancestors."

DEPRESSED LIKE ELIJAH?

Elijah was a prime candidate for depression. He was physically tired, he was emotionally exhausted, and somebody had threatened his life. He was an emotional fruit basket at this point, with all kinds of problems: fear, resentment, guilt, anger, loneliness, and worry. But God says that "Elijah was a man just like us" (James 5:17). He had the same problems we do, and in this case he had a problem with depression.

Elijah was so depressed that he was ready to die. Why do we get ourselves in such emotional messes? Because of *faulty thinking*. The fact is that *our emotions are caused by our thoughts.*

If you think in a negative way, you're going to feel depressed. Your emotions are caused by how you interpret life. If you look at life from a negative viewpoint you're going to get down.

If you want to get rid of negative emotions you have to change the way you think. The Bible says that you can be transformed by the *renewing of your mind* (Rom. 12:2). The only way you can change your mind and emotions is by changing the way you think. To overcome depression you've got to get your incorrect attitudes about life corrected. That's why Jesus said that when you "know the truth . . . the truth will set you free" (John 8:32). If you look at things from the right point of view, you will not be depressed.

FOCUS ON THE FACTS, NOT ON YOUR FEELINGS

Why did Elijah get depressed? Because he played four mental games that all of us play when we get depressed. The first one is found in verse 3: "Elijah was afraid and ran for his life." He came to a broom tree, sat under it, and prayed that he might die: "Lord, I've had enough. I'm fed up. I don't want to put up with it anymore. I'm just wasting my life. I'm trying to be Your servant, but nobody's doing what's right. I'm fed up; it's no use trying; I'm giving up."

What was his first mistake? The same mistake we make when we get depressed: *We focus on our feelings rather than on the facts.* That always happens when we're depressed. We focus on how we feel rather than on reality. Elijah felt like a failure because of one incident that frightened him. He thought to himself, "I'm such a coward—what am I doing running?" So because he *felt* like a failure, he assumed he *was* a failure.

This is called emotional reasoning, and it's destructive. It's the idea, "I feel it, so it must be true." Musicians, athletes, and TV stars, to name some, know that often after a performance they feel as though they've flopped. Yet they also know that they must learn to ignore those feelings because *feelings aren't always true.* Feelings are not facts; they are highly unreliable.

A few weeks after I had been married to Kay, one morning I woke up and said, "You know, Honey, I just don't feel married."

She replied, "It doesn't matter, Buddy. You are!"

I don't always feel close to God, either, but this doesn't necessarily mean that I'm far away from Him. I don't always feel like a Christian, but I am one. Feelings often lie, so when we focus on our feelings rather than on the facts, we're going to get into trouble. For instance, after we've made a mistake in one area we tend to feel we're total failures in life. That's a misconception. Everybody is entitled to make mistakes, and we can fail in one area without being a failure as a person.

Most psychologists believe that one key to health is to get your feelings out in the open. Become aware. Vent your feelings. Get them out. But that's not the complete answer, because feelings are unreliable. The Bible doesn't tell us to get in touch with our *feelings* but to get in touch with the *truth,* because it's the truth that sets us free.

DON'T COMPARE YOURSELF WITH OTHERS

The second mistake Elijah made is shown in the second thing he said: "I've had enough, Lord. Take my life, because I'm no better than my ancestors." A second mistake that causes depression is that *we start comparing ourselves with other people.* Most of us have fallen into the trap of thinking, "If I could just be like so-and-so, I'd be happy."

When you start comparing yourself with other people, you're asking for trouble. The Bible says it's unwise and harmful (2 Cor. 10:12). Don't compare yourself with somebody else, because everyone is unique. There's only one person that you can be, and that is *you*. If you're always trying to imitate other people and act like them, you're going to get depressed. The only person you can be is *you*. That's all God wants. That's all He expects.

When we start comparing ourselves with other people we fall into another trap: we tend to compare our weaknesses with other people's strengths, forgetting that those people also have weak areas that we might be strong in. We also try to motivate ourselves through criticism and condemnation. We do it by "shoulding" ourselves: "I should be able to be like that person. I should be able to act better. I should be able to accomplish it. I should be able to stop it"—as if whipping ourselves verbally is going to motivate us! Nagging doesn't work when you do it to another person, and self-criticism doesn't work either.

Recently my wife spoke at a Christian conference, and as I drove her there she made a profound statement: "We don't read the Bible to change God's opinion of us; we read the Bible to change our opinion of God." If I feel that I've got to read the Bible so God will like me, then reading the Bible becomes something I'm pressured to do, and we usually resist things we feel pressured to do. When somebody pushes at me my tendency is to push back. But when I realize that I read the Bible not to change God's opinion of me but to have my opinions about Him changed—understanding what He is like, how loving and gracious He is—then I *want* to read it.

Another trap we fall into when we get depressed is

that we label ourselves. Instead of saying, "I made a mistake," we say, "I'm a total failure." Instead of saying, "Oh, I accidentally tripped," we say, "I'm a klutz." Instead of saying, "I ate too much," we say, "I'm a pig." When we label ourselves with titles, it only reinforces our problems and makes things worse.

DON'T TAKE FALSE BLAME

The third mistake Elijah made was that he blamed himself for negative events that weren't his fault. Elijah said, "I have been very zealous for the Lord God Almighty. The Israelites have rejected Your covenant, broken down Your altars, and put Your prophets to death with the sword" (v. 10). He said, in effect, "I've worked hard for three years, but they're still not any closer to You. I've really tried, but they're still living the same way as before." In his depression Elijah blamed himself for failing to change the nation. He took it personally. A third mistake that causes depression is that *we take false blame*. When you do that you will always get depressed. If we assume a responsibility that God never intended us to have, it is too heavy a burden.

If you're in the habit of helping people, you sooner or later realize that people do not always respond the way you would like them to, whether it's your children or your friends or your spouse or people you work with. People react in many different ways. You can't assume responsibility for their responses.

God has given each of us a free will. When you assume responsibility for other people's decisions, you accept a burden that will only depress you. You can sometimes *influence* people, but you cannot *control* them.

The final decision is theirs. Don't be depressed by something you cannot control.

DON'T EXAGGERATE THE NEGATIVE

The fourth mistake Elijah made is that he exaggerated the negative. He said, "I am the only one left, and now they are trying to kill me too" (v. 10). Elijah held a little pity party for himself: "Everybody's against me." But the fact was that everybody was *not* against him. Only one person was violently against him, and her threat wasn't a real threat. If Elijah had just thought about it instead of listening to his feelings, he would have realized that Jezebel didn't dare kill him. True, the Queen sent a messenger with the threat, "Tomorrow I'm going to kill you." But if Jezebel had really intended to kill Elijah she wouldn't have sent a messenger to warn him; she would have just sent a hit man!

Jezebel was too clever to have Elijah killed. She recognized his powerful influence. If Elijah had been killed he would have become a martyr. That would have increased his influence and probably caused a revolution in the country. Besides that, she was probably afraid of what God would do to her if she touched His man. So her words were just a threat. She let him get away to the desert because she didn't really want to kill him. She just wanted to make him look like a coward in front of the nation.

But Elijah didn't stop to evaluate the threat. He just ran away. *When we're depressed we always exaggerate the negative.* Everything looks bad. If we're depressed, the whole world is going to pot. In actuality Elijah was *not* the only person still faithful to God. There were still

7,000 prophets who hadn't succumbed to the pagan religion (v. 18). Elijah exaggerated the problem, and it made his depression worse.

TAKE CARE OF YOUR PHYSICAL NEEDS

What was God's remedy for Elijah's depression? It was a remedy you can use for your depression. First, *take care of your physical needs.* We read that Elijah lay down under a tree and fell asleep. Then an angel touched him and said, "Get up and eat." He looked around, and there by his head was a cake of bread baked over hot coals and a jar of water. So he ate and drank, and went back to sleep.

Then the angel came a second time and said, "Get up and eat again, for the journey is too much for you." So he ate and drank, and was strengthened by that food (vv. 5-8).

God's initial remedy for Elijah's depression was rest, food, and relaxation. Sometimes a good night's sleep does wonders for your attitude. When you are physically tired and mentally drained, you're prone to depression. Notice how tenderly God dealt with Elijah. God did not scold him by saying, "You coward! What are you doing here in the desert?" God didn't put him down or condemn him; all God did was give him food and rest. God got him restored physically. That was the starting point. If you're depressed, the first step toward recovery is to get in shape physically. Take care of your health needs. Maybe you need to watch your diet or perhaps you need to get more sleep or begin an exercise program. Physical health has a profound influence on your moods.

GIVE YOUR FRUSTRATIONS TO GOD

The second remedy for your depression is to *give your frustrations to God.* Elijah then went into a cave and spent the night there. In the morning the Lord asked him, "What are you doing here, Elijah?"

He replied, "I've been zealous for the Lord God Almighty. Israel has rejected Your covenant, broken down Your altars, and put all Your prophets to death with the sword; I'm the only one left, and now they're trying to kill me too" (vv. 9-10). He just poured out all his inner feelings. God allowed him to let off steam. God was not shocked by Elijah's complaints.

God says, in effect, "When you're uptight, let Me hear your inner emotions. I already know what they are, and I'm not going to be shocked by them." He let Elijah vent his pent-up emotions without criticizing him or condemning him. Often it helps to share your feelings with a Christian friend. It's a catharsis—a cleansing out, a venting, of all the things that have been pushed down inside you and are causing your depression.

Notice the six emotions that Elijah felt. First, Elijah was *afraid* (v. 3). Then he felt *resentment* (v. 4). He said, "I'm fed up with it all, and I'm no better than my ancestors." He also had *low self-esteem* and felt *guilty.* Next Elijah complained that he worked hard for nothing (v. 10). He was *angry.* Then he said, "I'm all alone" (v. 10). He was *lonely.* Finally he added, "And they're trying to kill me too." He was *worried.* When you combine resentment, fear, guilt, anger, loneliness, and worry, you're asking for depression!

So God just let him spill this all out. He said, "Elijah, what's frustrating you? What's eating you up?" When you are depressed that's exactly what you need to do— tell it all to the Lord.

A FRESH AWARENESS OF GOD

The third remedy for your depression is to *get a fresh awareness of God's presence in your life*. The Lord told Elijah, "Go out and stand on the mountain in the presence of the Lord, for I am about to pass by" (v. 11). Then a powerful wind tore the mountains apart and shattered the rocks, but the Lord wasn't in the wind. After the wind came an earthquake, but the Lord wasn't in the earthquake either. After the earthquake came a fire, but the Lord wasn't in the fire either. After the fire came a gentle whisper, and when Elijah heard this he put his cloak over his face. He knew it was the Lord, so he went out and stood at the mouth of the cave.

God had put on a real show with the wind, earthquake, and fire, but He wasn't speaking to Elijah in any of those. What really got Elijah's attention was the still, small voice—the gentle whisper. Even today *God usually speaks to us in stillness and quietness*—not out of some big dramatic demonstration of fire or power. God reminded Elijah that He was still right there beside him.

If you are depressed, take your Bible and go to the ocean or to a lake or out in the country. Sit down and read your Bible, and get alone with God. Just let God love you and speak to you. Let Him meet your needs, and let yourself feel His presence. There is no greater antidepressant than communication and fellowship with God.

NEW DIRECTION FOR YOUR LIFE

The fourth remedy for overcoming depression is to *let God give you a new direction for your life*. The Lord told

Elijah, "Go back the way you came, and go to the
Desert of Damascus. When you get there, here's what I
want you to do" (v. 15). Then God gave Elijah a new
assignment. He put him back to work. The quickest way
to defeat depression is to quit sitting around in self-pity.
Get your eyes off yourself and start looking at the needs
of other people. Get involved in their lives in a ministry
where you are giving out and God is giving through
you. If you're constantly looking at yourself you'll get
discouraged. Jesus said, "Lose your life to find it"
(Matt. 16:25). Get involved in helping other people.

When we're depressed we tend to think, "How could
God ever use me? I'm such a failure. I keep making
mistakes. I disappoint myself, so surely I must be disap-
pointing God." *But you can never disappoint God,* because
disappointment can only happen when somebody expects you to do something different from what you
really do. The fact is that *God knows everything about you.*
He knows how you'll act in the future. So He's not
disappointed when it happens. God knows that you're
human, because He made you and He knows what
makes you tick.

Let God give you a new purpose and a new direction.
He's not through with you. You blew it? Big deal! If
you let Him, God will pick you up and start you over.
One mistake (or a hundred) does not make you useless
for life.

Jesus Christ wants to lift you out of your depression.
He can help you; He can change you; He can heal you
of depression. You don't have to go through life being
manipulated by your emotions. Your emotions are con-
trolled by your thoughts, and even though you cannot
directly control your emotions, you *can* control what
you think about. You *can* choose to change your

thoughts. Let God change those harmful misconceptions, such as: "If somebody criticizes me, it means I'm worthless." "I must be loved and accepted by *everybody* to be fulfilled in life." "I cannot admit any area of weakness; I have to be perfect or else I'm a failure." These are the kinds of misconceptions that cause depression. Jesus knew the importance of correct thinking when He said, "You will know the truth, and the truth will set you free" (John 8:32). The more you know Jesus, the freer you'll be.

YOU CAN CHANGE

You *can* change. How do you start? By establishing a personal relationship with Christ. You become what the Bible calls "born again." This doesn't automatically cure all your depression, but without Christ in your life you have no power to change. He wants to be a vital part of your life, and if you give Him control He will help you. Once He's in your life, ask Him to give you a new purpose and a new meaning in living. You need something greater to live for than just your own self. People who live for themselves are guaranteed to get depressed. You need something greater that draws you out of yourself, and that is a vital relationship with Christ, God's strong Son.

CHAPTER FOUR

How Can I Live Above Average?

God never meant for you to live a mediocre, average life. You are designed for excellence, and you were uniquely created. Instead of being one in a million, you're actually one in about five billion! There's nobody else like you; you are unique.

Everybody wants to be recognized. In fact, not only do you *want* to be recognized, but you *need* recognition, for the sake of your own emotional health. When my daughter Amy was very young, she would say to me, "Watch me, Daddy, watch me, Daddy!" She wanted to be recognized. She wanted to stand out from the crowd.

We as adults do the same thing, except that we don't do it as blatantly. But we do it with our cars and our clothing and our homes. All the time we're saying, "Watch me—everybody watch me!" We have a need in our lives to be different, to be excellent to stand out from everybody else.

STANDING OUT IN THE CROWD

First Chronicles 4:9-10 tells us about a man named Jabez. The first nine chapters of this book consist of genealogies, with a listing of over 600 names. Right in the middle of all these names God singles out one man for special recognition, and his name is Jabez.

There are only two verses in the entire Bible on this man, and yet he is given an honorable mention above 600 other people. Why did God say that this man lived above average? What did he do that caused his name to be preserved for over 4,000 years? "Jabez was *more honorable* than his brothers" (vv. 9-10). His mother named him Jabez "because I gave birth to him in pain."

Jabez prayed to God, "I want You to bless me and enlarge my territory! Let Your hand be with me, and keep me from harm so that I will be free from pain." And God granted his request.

GREAT AMBITIONS

There were three secrets to this man's life—three principles that can make your life above average too. First, Jabez had a great ambition. While all his friends were content with being average and mediocre, Jabez said, "I want God to bless me. I want something big. I want to do something significant with my life." He didn't want to be ordinary. He didn't want to be common. He wanted to expand and grow. He said, "God, bless me and enlarge my land." Jabez had a great ambition—and most deeply of all he wanted God's blessing on his life. Many people today just drift through life. They have no goals, no master plan, no overall purpose, and no ambition. As a result they never accomplish much. They simply exist.

The first principle of living above average is that *you need a great ambition.* You need a dream. If you don't have a dream, you're drifting. When you stop dreaming, you start dying. When you stop setting goals, you stop growing. You've got to have something that you're pushing toward, a goal of excellence. As long as your horizon is expanding, you'll be an emotionally healthy human being. God made you for growth; He wants you to grow and stretch and develop. God has a purpose for your life, and your key to success is to discover that purpose and cooperate with it. God never intended for you to go through life with a halfhearted attitude, wondering what you're doing and where you're going. God wants you to have a great ambition. A life with no challenges and no goals can be summed up in one word: boredom.

There are three common misconceptions that keep us from having great ambitions. The first misconception is that *we confuse humility with fear.* We say, "Oh, I could never do that," and we think we're being humble. But that's not true humility. That's *fear; that's a lack of faith.* A really humble person would say, "With God's help I can do it. With God's blessing I *will* do it. I may not be able to do it on my own, but with God's help I will do it." That's true humility.

Second, *we tend to confuse contentment with laziness.* It's true that Paul said, "I have learned to be content whatever the circumstances" (Phil. 4:11). But this doesn't mean that you shouldn't set any goals. Paul was *not* saying, "I've learned to not set any goals, and I don't have any ambitions or any future desires." He was saying, "Even though my goals may not be reached yet,

I've learned to enjoy today to the fullest. I'm happy today even though I have dreams and ambitions that haven't been fulfilled yet." If contentment were used as an excuse for laziness, who would ever feed the poor or worry about world hunger and equality and justice? How would anyone ever get an education? A third-grade kid would say, "I've learned to be content with the third grade," and he wouldn't go any farther. We must not confuse contentment with laziness.

Third, we confuse small thinking with spirituality. People have said to me, "I serve God in my little way."

My reply is, "Well, why don't you start serving Him in a bigger way? Let God use you more!"

Other people say, "Well, I'm just the way I am. That's the way God made me." But it's wrong to blame God for our lack of growth. Don't confuse small thinking with spirituality.

GROWING FAITH

The second principle for living above average is you need a growing faith. Not only did Jabez have a great ambition, but he also had a growing faith. He had a deep trust and belief in God. He had enough faith to pray and expect an answer. He was like William Carey, who said, "Attempt great things for God; expect great things from God."

The Bible gives us some interesting facts about Jabez. First, there's no mention of Jabez having any special ability or talent or gift. The Bible doesn't say that he was wealthy or educated. He was simply a common man with an uncommon faith. Don't worry about what you *don't* have if you *do* have faith! God will give you the necessary power. God loves to use ordinary people who believe in Him, who are willing to trust Him.

Jabez's faith caused him to believe that God would help him with his goals and his dreams. There is something more important than being talented, more important than ability or education—it's *faith.* It's believing that God will work through you. I've met many super-talented people who are sitting on the sidelines while ordinary people with faith are making the touchdowns. They believe God, so He uses them. Like Jabez, they're just ordinary people with extraordinary faith.

Another thing is that Jabez apparently had some type of handicap or disability. In the Hebrew language "Jabez" means "painful." How would you like to be named "Painful"? "Here comes Painful," or "There's old Painful over there." Jabez caused his mother so much grief when he was born that she named him Painful. He may have been unwanted and unloved. His name constantly reminded him that even his birth caused grief in someone else's life. But Jabez was stronger than this handicap. His faith kept him going.

Regardless of his past painful experiences he had the faith to look ahead and to attempt great things in the future.

What is your handicap? Is it physical? Is it spiritual? Is it an unhappy childhood? Is it a frustrating job or problem in marriage? Whatever it may be, God says, *"Everything is possible for him who believes"* (Mark 9:23).

GENUINE PRAYER

The third secret to Jabez's life was his prayer life. It was Jabez's simple prayer request that got him an honorable mention in the Bible, and we're still talking about him thousands of years later.

Maybe you've hesitated to ask for things in prayer. Maybe you've felt your request was selfish. What kind of prayer does God answer? The life of Jabez illustrates three things we can ask God for and expect Him to answer.

The first thing Jabez prayed for was *God's power in his life.* He asked for a power greater than his own to accomplish his dream. He prayed, "I want You to bless me. I want Your power in my life."

It is important that Jabez's request was most specific: "God, this is what I want You to do: I want You to enlarge my coast; I want You to expand my territory; I want more real estate."

Do you pray about your goals? Do you ask God to help you wherever you're headed in your life? The third principle for living above average is *you need a genuine prayer life*. At first glance Jabez's prayer seems selfish, doesn't it? He prayed, "God, I want You to do all these things for me."

But evidently God approved of the prayer, because He answered it. Here is the point: *Ambition is neither good nor bad; it's just a basic drive in life.* Everybody has some ambition. It may be great or small, but everybody has some ambition in life. Maybe your ambition is just to get up in the morning, but you've got to have some ambition to live in the world.

What makes ambition good or bad? One thing: the *motive* behind it. And Jabez's motives were genuine because God never honors an unworthy request. Consider this: *God dares you to ask for big requests*. What do you ask God for when you pray? God encourages you to ask: "You do not have, because you do not ask God"

(James 4:2). Jeremiah says, "Call to Me and I will answer you, and tell you great and unsearchable things you do not know" (Jer. 33:3). Paul says that God "is able to do immeasurably more than all we ask or imagine, according to His power that is at work within us" (Eph. 3:20). This means that you cannot out-ask God. You cannot out-dream God. If you could stretch your imagination to the greatest limits of what you think could possibly happen, God can go beyond even that. He can go beyond *your* imagination. God says, "Trust Me. Ask things. Get a great ambition, then get a growing faith, then bring them to Me in genuine prayer."

What do you want God to do in your life? Heal a bad marriage situation? Ask Him. Help you with a problem? Ask Him. Help you with some goals? Ask Him. God is not some big policeman up in the sky waiting for you to make one wrong move so He can pounce on you; God *wants* to bless your life.

The second thing Jabez prayed for was *God's presence in his life:* "Let Your hand be with me" (1 Chron. 4:10). Jabez realized, "If I get more territory, that means I'll have more responsibility. I'll have greater demands and more pressure, and I'll really need God's help in my life. So he requested God to be with him. When you ask for God's presence in your life, you can be sure He will answer.

The third thing Jabez prayed for was *God's protection over his life:* "Keep me from harm so that I will be free from pain" (v. 10). He asked God for His protection. Why did Jabez do that? Because in those days, the more land you had, the more influence you had, and the better-known you were.

It's still true today: *The more successful you are, the more critics you have.* The more territory you own, the more enemies will attack you. The closer you grow to the Lord and the stronger you become as a Christian, the more the devil will harass you, because he doesn't want you to grow. But you can be sure, as Jabez was, that with God's protection you don't have to fear anyone or anything.

If you combine the three requests that Jabez prayed for, I guarantee that you'll live above average. Do you want to break out of mediocrity? Do you want to see God work in your life? Do you want to see real answers to your prayers? Are you tired of drifting through life not knowing where you're going?

If you really want to live above average, if you want God's best for your life, then follow these three principles that Jabez used: get a great ambition, a glimpse of what God wants to do in your life; get a growing faith in God, a faith that enables you to expect the impossible; establish a genuine prayer life, one that depends on God as you work toward your dream.

How Can I Have Peace of Mind?

We live in a very tense, uptight world. This has been called the age of anxiety. We all face situations that make us irritable and tense and rob us of peace of mind. A major cause of heart attacks and high blood pressure is tension and stress. Every year over 500 million dollars' worth of tranquilizers are prescribed to drop people into emotional low gear.

Most tension is really the result of unresolved conflict. If you have an argument with somebody at work, you'll be tense until you talk it out. Unresolved issues also create tension in your life. If you have a major decision to make, and you can't seem to decide what to do about it, it's upsetting and frustrating.

THE MAN OF INNER PEACE

Moses was a man who learned how to resolve the basic issues of life, and as a result became a prime example of how to enjoy peace of mind. Because he made the right decisions, and settled what is important in life, he was able to live with himself and assume a tremendous responsibility, and yet remain calm under pressure. I think Moses was the greatest man of faith in the Old Testament. In Hebrews 11, "God's Hall of Fame" of great men and women of faith, Moses gets more coverage than anyone else. Moses knew how to be at peace with himself, how to enjoy inner peace of mind.

Yet if anybody had a right to be uptight, it was Moses. He had a dream of leading two million Israelites out of the land of Egypt, across the desert and into a new country called Israel, the Promised Land. It was a great, God-inspired dream. But for nearly the entire time the people complained, argued, and fought. They just didn't have enough faith to enter the Promised Land, so they spent forty years wandering around the wilderness, until all the original adults died off. Then their children were allowed to go in. Moses never got to see his dream fulfilled because of the faithlessness of his people.

He had a right to be uptight, but the Bible tells us that Moses was a meek man. Now "meek" does not mean "weak." Meekness is an attitude of quiet confidence, of inner tranquility and peace of mind. Meekness keeps you from getting ruffled when things get hot. Meekness is the attitude that says, "When everybody's coming down on me, when everybody's on my case, when things are uptight and I have every legitimate reason to get nervous and tense, I'm going to be cool. I'm not going to lose my temper." Only two people in the entire Bible were called meek: Jesus and Moses. Moses is a prime example of how to enjoy peace of mind.

THE FOUR ISSUES OF LIFE

Why was Moses able to have this peace of mind? Why was he able to be at peace with himself? Because *Moses was a man of great principles.* Every decision he made was based on fundamental principles of life. He did not live by his feelings; instead, he based his life on God's principles for living. "God doesn't want us to build our lives around petty rules, but around great principles." Moses came to grips with four fundamental issues of life that each of us eventually face.

Whether you are a teenager or a senior citizen or somewhere in between, each of us eventually has to deal with these fundamental issues. If you can learn to settle these issues in your mind, you'll learn what it means to have real peace of mind. You'll learn how to be calm in a crisis, how to be strong under stress, and how to be at peace under pressure.

"By faith Moses' parents hid him for three months after he was born because they saw that he was no ordinary child and because they were not afraid of the king's edict" (Heb. 11:23). (The Pharaoh of Egypt had proclaimed that every newborn Jewish boy in the land of Egypt was to be killed.) By faith Moses, when he had grown up, refused to be known as the son of Pharaoh's daughter. He chose to be mistreated along with the people of God rather than to enjoy the pleasures of sin for a short time. He regarded this sacrifice for the sake of Christ as of greater value than the treasures of Egypt, because he was looking ahead to his reward. By faith he left Egypt, not fearing the Pharaoh's anger.

We read in Hebrews 11 that Moses dealt with four questions. First he settled the question, "Who am I?" (v. 24) Next he settled the question, "What do I really want to be?" (v. 25) Then he settled the question,

"What is really important in life?" (v. 26) And finally he settled the question, "How am I going to live?" (v. 27) These are four fundamental, bedrock issues that you need to come to grips with. In every one of these crucial issues, Moses responded in the right way. He made the correct decision, and as a result we honor him today.

KNOW WHO YOU ARE

The first thing Moses dealt with (v. 24) is the issue of *identity*. He settled the issue of "Who am I?" Moses, when he grew up, refused to be known as the son of Pharaoh's daughter. Pharaoh had proclaimed that every newborn Jewish boy should be killed, but his mother hid him in a little basket in the reeds of the Nile River. Pharaoh's daughter came along to bathe, and she found this little tar-lined crib floating, and in it this little Jewish boy. Immediately she fell in love with the baby, took him home with her, and raised him right there in the Egyptian palace.

We need to understand the conflict here. Moses was actually a Jew, but Pharaoh's daughter raised him as an Egyptian. Everybody thought he was a bona fide Egyptian.

Years later, at about the age of forty, he was being groomed to be second in command in the kingdom, so he had to make a choice: "What am I going to do with my life? I know I'm a Jew, but nearly everybody thinks I'm an Egyptian."

Moses had every comfort he could wish for in the palace, and he could have stayed there. But he had an identity crisis: "Who am I? Am I a Jew or am I an

Egyptian? Am I going to live with a bunch of Jewish slaves, or am I going to stay here and live in luxury in the palace?" What would you have done? Moses made the right decision regarding this issue of identity, but it cost him the next eighty years of his life in the desert.

Every one of us must come to grips with this issue of identity. We all have a deep need to accept who we are.

If you try to be somebody you're really not, it's a quick way to an ulcer, because the pressure is on. Moses recognized this tension, and he decided to quit pretending. He accepted his true identity.

It is a liberating experience when you relax and quit trying to be somebody you're not. The foundation for peace of mind is *Don't try to be someone you're not.* Relax and be yourself. God made you, and He loves you just the way that you are, warts and all. You're special to Him.

You can pretend to be someone else or you can accept God's plan and be who you were really meant to be in the first place. How would we remember Moses today if he had stayed in Pharaoh's court? Maybe as an Egyptian mummy in some museum. But he made the hard decision, and in the light of eternity it was the best one.

Several years ago Anne Murray came out with a hit song, "You Needed Me." There's one phrase that says, "You lifted me up and gave me dignity." That's what Jesus Christ does for us.

God not only gives us an identity, but He gives us *dignity* along with it. Every person Jesus dealt with in the New Testament—whether the woman caught in adultery or a leper or an outcast—was accepted and loved by Jesus. He said, "I know your name. You're a person." When you quit trying to be somebody you're not, you can relax and let God work in your life.

ACCEPT YOUR RESPONSIBILITIES

There's another issue that Moses dealt with, the matter of *personal responsibility*. The Bible says that Moses chose to be mistreated with the rest of God's people rather than to enjoy the sinful pleasures of Pharaoh's palace (v. 25). First he *refused to be* what he really wasn't, and then he *chose* to go God's way. The principle is this: You can always replace a negative with a positive. You don't just stop doing something; you start doing something else. The Christian life is not a matter of negative rules and regulations; it's a matter of relationships—with God, with others, and with yourself. Someone has joked, "If all the Christian life consisted of was a list of don'ts, then everyone who is dead would qualify as a Christian!" But God's way is a positive way.

Notice something else: Moses made his decision "when he had grown up" (Heb. 11:24). It's a mark of maturity when you settle the issue of personal responsibility. When Moses was a baby it was OK for him to postpone the decision about who he was. But when he became an adult he had to decide, "Who am I?" He had to make a choice, to assume responsibility for his own life, and to move ahead.

The truth of personal responsibility is an unpopular truth in our society today. We live in a culture that loves to blame others and not accept personal responsibility. Who was responsible for the 1973 oil crisis? The Americans blamed the Arabs, the Arabs blamed the oil companies, the oil companies blamed the U.S. government, and the government blamed the ecologists. Nobody wanted to accept any blame.

All of us love to *give* blame but we all hate to *be* blamed. It's easy to blame others for your condition: "I'd be more committed to Christ if my family were Christians." "I'd really go God's way if my boyfriend or girlfriend or mother or father or husband or wife would get going." "I'd be a better person today if I had better parents." Moses didn't blame anyone else: he assumed the responsibility for his own life and decided to make his life count.

It is true, of course, that there are many things in your life over which you have no control. You had no control over who your parents were. You had no control over where you were born. You had no control over the genes that went into your makeup. But there is one thing which you have absolute control over, and that is *your response* toward life. You can choose to respond toward life in a negative, critical manner, or you can choose to respond toward life in a positive manner of faith.

How are you going to respond? It's your choice. You cannot choose all the circumstances that come into your life, but you *can* choose whether those things will make you a bitter person or a better person. It's your responsibility. *No one can ruin your life except you!* The devil can't, because he doesn't have enough power. God won't, because He loves you. Only *you* can ruin your own life.

But what about other people? Don't they do things to you? Yes, but you choose how you respond to them. A survivor of a German concentration camp said the only thing he learned was that, though he could not control what happened to him, he *could* control how he responded to it. Nobody can take away your attitude unless you give it away. When you assume responsibility for your own attitude, then you can start enjoying true peace of mind.

② DECIDE YOUR PRIORITIES

There's another issue that Moses faced. He chose to be mistreated along with the people of God rather than to enjoy the pleasures of sin for a short time (v. 25). He regarded this sacrifice for the sake of Christ as of greater value than the treasures of Egypt. Moses faced the issue of *priorities*. He decided what was really important in life.

From the human standpoint young Moses had everything. He had ultimate power, ultimate pleasure, and ultimate possessions. Much of the riches of the world at that time were stored in Egypt. Moses had what most people spend their entire lives trying to get: power, pleasure, and possessions.

Yet God asked Moses to do something that was more important, so he did it. It was a matter of priority in his life. Because Moses was considered the son of Pharaoh's daughter and was in a position of great power, he could have rationalized, "The slave situation is bad, so I'll just stay in the system and work for reform."

But God didn't say that. He told Moses, "Get out there and get moving!"

Most people want to be liked in their community, but there's one problem with popularity: it never lasts. You can be a Big Man on Campus for a while, but when you return a few years after graduation you'll find that nobody knows you. Popularity just doesn't last.

Then there's always pleasure. Is pleasure wrong? No,

it's not wrong to have pleasure unless it's your god. But we live in a pleasure-possessed society: "You only go around once in life, so you'd better do it with gusto." "Do your own thing." "If it feels good, do it." But there's a problem with pleasure too: It doesn't last either. Moses rejected temporary pleasures because he had his values right; he had his vision on something higher.

There's nothing inherently wrong with having money. Some of the greatest saints of the Bible were extremely wealthy, including Job, Abraham, and David. But the Bible says that a man's life does not consist in the abundance of things he possesses (Luke 12:15). Wealth simply will not bring ultimate happiness: Ask the people who have it. How much money does it take to be happy? Usually just a little bit more. *Money is to be used, not loved.* God wants you to use things and love people. But if you love things, you'll use people. Moses had his priorities right; he rejected material things because there was something more important in his life.

④ *FACE YOUR DIFFICULTIES*

The final issue Moses settled was the matter of perseverance. You could almost sum up Moses' life in two words: he endured (Heb. 11:27, KJV). It is a fact of life that there is no gain without pain, no advancement without adversity, no progress without problems. On the issue of endurance, learn how to relate to difficulties.

Moses made a success of his life because he *endured.* The key to his peace of mind was that he knew difficulties come into every life, and he knew how to respond to them correctly and move on. As Christians we should never let problems destroy us; we should let problems draw us closer to God. Somebody has said that a Christian should never let problems get him down, except down on his knees. God allows these situations in our lives for specific reasons.

Without persistence you won't go far in life. Peace of mind comes when you accept responsibility for choices in your life, choose God's priorities, and then confidently persevere.

CHAPTER SIX

How Can I Handle Discouragement?

What can you do when you have the world's deadliest disease? No, it's not cancer, not polio, not MS, and not AIDS. It's *discouragement.*

Why is discouragement such a dreaded disease? First, because it's universal. All of us get discouraged. I do, you do, we all do. Discouragement is common. Even Christians get discouraged. Second, because it's recurring. You can get discouragement a number of times. It's not just a one-time thing. Third, because it's highly contagious. Other people can get discouraged because *you're* discouraged.

NOW THE GOOD NEWS

But the good news is that discouragement is also curable. A story from the life of Nehemiah (chap. 4) illustrates four causes and three cures for discouragement.

You recall that the man Nehemiah was a leader of the Jewish group that had returned to Israel from Babylon to rebuild the wall around Jerusalem. When they had first started on the wall, they had had a lot of fervor and zeal and were very excited about the project. But after working awhile they got discouraged.

Chapter 4 of Nehemiah shows why people get discouraged and how to overcome that discouragement—what to do when you feel like giving up. "So we rebuilt the wall until all of it reached half its height, for the people worked with all their heart" (4:6). Verses 10-12 continue: "Meanwhile, the people in Judah said, The strength of the laborers is giving out, and there is so much rubble that we cannot rebuild the wall. Also our enemies said, Before they know it or see us, we will be right there among them and will kill them and put an end to the work. Then the Jews who live near them came and told us ten times over, Wherever you turn, they will attack us."

JUST PLAIN TIRED

Why do people get discouraged? The first reason is *fatigue.* The people in Judah said, "The strength of the laborers is giving out." In other words, they had worked a long time and were physically exhausted. They were just plain worn out—physically and emotionally drained.

Sometimes people come to me for counseling who incorrectly think that their discouragement is a spiritual problem. They say, "Maybe I just need to recommit my life to the Lord." But their real problem is that they're just burned out. They just need some rest, relaxation, and renewal. So I tell them, "You don't need to recommit your life—you just need some rest." Sometimes the most spiritual thing you can do is just go to bed and relax, or take an affordable two-week vacation.

When do fatigue and discouragement come about? Look at verse 6: "So we rebuilt the wall till all of it reached half its height." Do you know when you're apt to get discouraged the most? When you're halfway through a project. Everybody works hard at first. These people "worked with all their heart" (v. 6). Why? Because of the newness of the project. It was novel at first, but after awhile the newness wore off and the work got boring. Life settled down into a rut, then a routine, then a ritual.

Have you ever painted a room? You get halfway through it and then look around and say, "Man, I'm getting tired, and I'm just half-finished. Not only that, but after I'm finished I've got to clean everything up."

I did a fatiguing thing not long ago. I tried to reorganize my filing cabinets. Do you know what it means to clean out your filing cabinets? It means that you take all the things out of your file, then put them in different piles all over the floor; then you get discouraged and put everything back the way it was!

Have you ever started to climb a mountain and thought, "It'll only take me four hours to get to the top"? But when you're halfway to the top you've already spent five hours! So you think, "Shall I keep going? I've got to go that far back down again too!" Suddenly you start thinking, "Maybe it's God's will that I go back down." Fatigue is the number one cause of discouragement, and it often happens right about the midpoint. That's why so many people seldom complete anything.

OVERCOMING FRUSTRATION

But there's a second reason why people get discouraged. The people said, "There is so much rubble that we cannot build the wall" (v. 10). That's *frustration*. They were discouraged and frustrated. What's rubble? They were building a new wall, but old broken rocks were everywhere, along with dirt and dried-out mortar. When they looked at the rubble and the debris they got discouraged. They lost sight of their goal because there was so much junk in their lives that they didn't know how to get to the real business of living.

Whenever you do a project some waste is going to accumulate, and it can get to be pretty frustrating. Have you ever expanded a room or constructed a building? All of a sudden you notice piles of plaster all over the place. Or you paint a room, and there's more paint everywhere else than on the walls! The trash just seems to multiply. You can't avoid rubbish in life, but you *can* learn to recognize it and you *can* learn what to do with it so you don't give up on your original plan.

What is the rubbish in your life? It's the trivial things that waste your time and consume your energy and frustrate you, that keep you from becoming all you want to be, that keep you from doing the things that are really most important in life. The rubbish in your life is those things that get in your way, the interruptions that keep you from accomplishing your goals. These are the things we need to clean away in our lives.

MAKING FAILURE TEMPORARY

The third reason why people get discouraged is also covered in verse 10: "We cannot rebuild the wall." Do you know what they were saying? "We can't do it. It's impossible. It's foolish to try. We give up." The third cause of discouragement is *failure.* The people were unable to finish their task as quickly as they had originally planned, and as a result their confidence went down the tubes. They lost heart and got discouraged. They said, "We can't do it, so we're just going to give up."

How do you handle failure in your life? Do you have a pity party? Do you say, "Oh, poor me. I can't get this job done"? Do you start complaining? "It's impossible. It can't be done. I was a fool to even try. It's stupid."

Or do you blame other people? "Everybody else let me down. They didn't do their parts of the job." The difference between winners and losers is that winners always see failure as being only a temporary setback.

STOPPED BY FEAR?

There's a fourth reason why people get discouraged. Nehemiah's people put it this way: "Our enemies said, Before they know it or see us, we will be right there among them and will kill them and put an end to the work" (v. 11). There were people in the land of Israel who did not want the wall to be built; they were the enemies of the Jews. A wall around the city represented safety and defense, so these enemies did not want the wall to be finished. So first they criticized the Jews, then they ridiculed them, and finally they threatened them: "We're going to kill you if you keep on building the wall." So the wall-builders got discouraged. Why? Because of the fourth cause of discouragement, *fear.*

Notice who it was that got discouraged. It was "the

Jews who lived near" the enemy, (v. 12). Then they discouraged others by saying, "Wherever you turn, they will attack us." When you hang around a negative person long enough, you know what happens. You pick up his negativism too. If you hear somebody keep saying, "It can't be done," you'll start believing him.

Do you have fears that are discouraging you right now—fears that are preventing you from developing and growing? Do you fear criticism or embarrassment? Are you afraid to take the big step and get the new job? Maybe it's a fear that you're not capable for the task. Maybe it's a fear that you can't hold up under the pressure. Maybe it's a fear that you have to be perfect. Fear *always discourages you.*

How can you tell if your discouragement is being caused by fear? You have a deep, intense desire to run: "I've got to get out of this place!" You have an intense desire to escape from life's demands and pressures. The natural reaction of fear is always to run. In life there are only three ways you can move—*against* something in anger, *away* from it in fear, or *with* it in love.

What is the antidote to this terrible disease of discouragement? Notice what Nehemiah did as a wise leader and a man of God. He knew what it was that discouraged people, so he took the appropriate actions to correct the problem. There are three principles to help you when you feel like giving up, and here they are in a nutshell: *Reorganize, remember,* and *resist.*

FIND A BETTER WAY

Nehemiah used the *reorganize* principle: "Therefore I stationed some of the people behind the lowest points of the wall at the exposed places, posting them by families, with their swords, spears, and bows" (v. 13). Nehemiah said, "We're going to get this thing really organized. We're going to get a new system here. You people go over there, and you other people stand here, and we'll get this problem solved."

The first principle in conquering discouragement is this: *Reorganize your life.* When you get discouraged, *don't give up on your goals. Instead, devise a new approach.* When you get discouraged, it doesn't necessarily mean that you're doing the wrong thing; you can be doing the right thing in the wrong way. Was it wrong for these Jews to be building the wall? Absolutely not; it was the right thing. But they were doing the right thing in the wrong way, and as a result they got discouraged.

Do you have a problem? Reorganize your life. A problem in your marriage? Don't give up on it. Try a new attitude. A problem in your business? Don't give up on it. Try a new approach. A problem in your Christian living? Don't give up on it. Try a new prayer. A problem with your health? Try a new doctor. Just *don't give up. Keep on keeping on.*

Some of you are discouraged because you are under tremendous pressure; your work load is unbelievable. God's message to you is *reorganize.* Reorganize your time; reorganize your schedule; refocus on your goal. Clear out the clutter and rubble and trivia, the things that are wasting your time. Then reorganize so you work toward your main goal.

Not long ago I was reminded at a seminar of the 80/20 principle: About 80 percent of our time is usually spent on the 20 percent of our activities that are not productive. As a result we are frustrated. What we need to do instead is spend 80 percent of our time on the 20 percent of our job that produces the most results. Managers call this ROI time—"Return On Investment" time. In other words, use the maximum time on those few things that get the greatest results.

Small group

Notice that Nehemiah focused on priorities. When he reorganized, he posted the people by families. Why? Because he knew that anybody who is discouraged needs a support group. We need other people, and families are a natural group. When one person in a family gets discouraged, other members will lift him up. We need our fellow Christians to support each other and encourage each other. When I get down, you lift me up, and when you get down, I lift you up. That's a support group.

Solomon says, "Two are better than one, because they have a good return for their work: if one falls down, his friend can help him up. But pity the man who falls and has no one to help him up! Also, if two lie down together, they will keep warm. But how can one keep warm alone? Though one may be overpowered, two can defend themselves. And a cord of three strands is not quickly broken" (Ecc. 4:9-12). What is he saying? That it is important to have other people in our lives in order to help us and encourage us.

REMEMBER YOUR LEADER

How else do you overcome discouragement? By remembering your Lord. Notice what Nehemiah said: "After I looked things over, I stood up and said to the nobles, the officials, and the rest of the people, 'Don't be afraid of them. *Remember the Lord,* who is great and awesome' " (Neh. 4:14). What does it mean to "remember the Lord"? It means to recommit yourself to Him. It means to rededicate yourself to Him. It means to draw on His spiritual power.

What specifically do you remember? Three things. First, remember God's goodness to you in the past. When you start thinking about all the good things that God has already done in your life, your spirit will be lifted. Second, remember God's closeness in the present. What is God doing in your life right now? He is with you whether you feel Him or not, because He said, "Never will I leave you; never will I forsake you" (Heb. 13:5). You may not be calling on God, but He is still there. Third, remember God's power for the future— He will give you strength for your needs. "I can do everything through" Christ, because He strengthens me (Phil. 4:13). When you get discouraged, get your mind off your circumstances and on the Lord. For, circumstances depress and discourage.

Remember, your thoughts determine your feelings. If you feel discouraged it's because you're thinking discouraging thoughts. If you want to feel encouraged instead, start thinking encouraging thoughts. Choose some uplifting Bible verses to memorize: "I can do all things through Christ, who strengthens me" (Phil. 4:13, KJV). Nothing can separate me "from the love of God" (Rom. 8:39). "If God is for us, who can be against us?" (Rom. 8:31) "Everything is possible for him who believes" (Mark 9:23).

FIGHT THE GLOOMY OUTLOOK

How else do you fight discouragement? By resisting the discouragement. Notice what Nehemiah says: "Fight for your brothers, your sons and your daughters, your wives and your homes'' (Neh. 4:14b). What is Nehemiah saying? "Don't yield to discouragement without a fight. *Resist discouragement.* Fight it. Don't give in to it, but resist it."

The Bible teaches that we who are Christians are in a spiritual warfare, a battle. We are in a supernatural conflict, a combat with negative forces. The Bible says that the devil is the accuser of Christians; he loves to get us down. That is his number one tool, because he knows that a discouraged Christian has limited potential. He knows that when we're down, our effectiveness is neutralized. So he does everything he can to discourage us. James says, "Resist the devil" (James 4:7). Resist him and his negative thoughts—all the discouragement he tries to bring into your life.

You do not have to be discouraged in life. It's your choice. You may choose to give in to it. But great people simply refuse to be discouraged. They don't know how to quit. They never give up even when they're fatigued and frustrated and have failed and are fearful. Great people are ordinary people with extraordinary amounts of persistence. They just hang in there and never give up.

How Can I Overcome My Problems?

The best known story of Jehoshaphat describes one of the great epic battles in the life of Israel. It is relevant to each of us because we all face battles each day: financial battles, spiritual battles, employment battles—all kinds of battles in our daily lives. God put the story of Jehoshaphat in the Bible in order to illustrate certain vital spiritual principles in winning the battles of life.

Jehoshaphat, king of Israel, got word from a friend that three enemy nations were coming against him to fight him. The odds weren't too good because it was three nations against the one nation of Israel. The chronicler tells us that these three nations were the Moabites, the Ammonites, and the Meunites (2 Chron. 20:1).

IDENTIFY THE ENEMY

Verse 1 shows us the first principle in overcoming the battles of life: *Identify the enemy.* This seems like a rather obvious principle, but actually it isn't. Many people simply do not know who their enemy is. Often we think the enemy is some other person who is trying to get our job or somebody else in our family, but many times the enemy is *our own attitude:* It's not so much the *situation* that gets us down but *our response to the situation.* Before we can start winning our personal battles, we have to accurately and honestly identify the enemy.

Notice how Jehoshaphat reacted (v. 3) when he heard that these three nations were coming against him: he was alarmed. That's a typical reaction for all of us. When we see a problem we say, "What's going to happen to me? I'm starting to get afraid!" This is a natural reaction to problems and fear is not wrong unless we deal with it in the wrong way. If we use fear to motivate ourselves to conquer the problem, that's fine. But if we get discouraged and give up, or else get angry with God and say, "Why me?" then fear defeats us.

TAKE IT TO THE LORD

Jehoshaphat became afraid because he faced an apparently hopeless situation. So what did he do? He proclaimed a fast and had all the people come together to seek help from the Lord (vv. 3-4). People came from every town in Judah to seek the Lord. The second principle in winning the battles of life is to *take your problems to the Lord.* Prayer ought to be the *first* weapon we use whenever we face the battles of life, not the last.

A deacon came to his pastor one day and said, "Pastor, we've really got a problem. Nothing's happening, and we can't solve the problem."

The pastor said, "Well, I guess all we can do is pray

about it."

The deacon replied, "Pastor, has it come to that?" Usually the last thing we try is prayer, because we want to work things out on our own. Just remember that Jesus fought the biggest battles in life, and He also prayed the most.

Jehoshaphat prayed, in effect, "God, I know You've helped me in the past. I know You can help me in the future. So please help me *now*." He continued, "Please judge our enemies, for we have no power to face this vast army that is attacking us. We don't know what to do, but our eyes are upon You" (vv. 6-12).

ADMIT YOUR INADEQUACY

The third principle in winning the battles of life is to *admit your inadequacy*. You need to say, "Lord, I've got a problem, and I need Your help with it." There's only one kind of person that God doesn't help, and that's a person who doesn't think he needs help. When you say, "Lord, I've got a problem; I need help, I admit my inadequacy," then He can work on it. The Christian life is a supernatural life, and we need God's power to live it. We can't live it on our own because we have a power shortage. We live the Christian life "not by might nor by power, but by [God's] Spirit" (Zech. 4:6). We need to let God's Spirit live through us.

RELY ON GOD'S RESOURCES

After Jehoshaphat admitted, "Lord, I don't know what to do," he added, "but our eyes are upon You"

(2 Chron. 20:12). The fourth principle in overcoming life's battles is to *rely on God's resources*. We need to get our eyes on the Lord. Too often we've got our eyes on everything else—on everything except the One who can solve our problems. Circumstances are like a mattress: If we're on top, we rest easy, but if we're underneath, we might suffocate. If we keep our eyes on the Lord we'll stay on top of our circumstances.

RELAX IN FAITH

Notice how God responded to Jehoshaphat's prayer: "Don't be afraid or discouraged because of this vast army, for the battle is not yours but God's" (v. 15). The fifth principle in overcoming life's battles is to *relax in faith*. So many Christians today are totally worn out because they're trying to fight God's battles in their own strength. When we try to fight God's battles in our own power, we're sure to get defeated.

When we first become Christians we tend to think, "God, You don't know what a deal You got when You got me. I'm going to bring in Your kingdom single-handedly. I'll go out and win the world and really help You." So we work real hard but eventually come crawling back on our hands and knees saying, "Lord, I know I've really disappointed You. I'm so sorry. I've really let You down."

But God replies, "No, you didn't let Me down, because you weren't holding Me up." *We don't hold up God; He holds us up. We don't have God in our hands; He has us in His hands.* God is trying to tell us, "Relax in faith and let Me work through you."

There was a time in my life as a Christian when I had

been working real hard for the Lord, doing it all under my own power. And I got so tired. Finally I was really griping to God one night, just kind of complaining. I said, "Lord, this stinks. God, I don't like it. I'm tired. I'm sick and tired. In fact, I'm sick and tired of being sick and tired." Then I said, "God I give up." I didn't know what to expect—I didn't know if that was really going to shock Him or something.

Then I heard this voice saying, "Great. Now I can start working, because as long as you're out there trying to make your own plans and do it on your own you're just going to mess it up. Relax—let Me work through you."

Paul says, "As you *received* Christ Jesus as Lord, *continue to live in Him*" (Col. 2:6). In other words, just the way you *became* a believer, be sure to *live* the Christian life the same way. You didn't become a Christian by working real hard, by promising to be perfect, by doing your very best. The Bible says that salvation is not of works, lest any man should boast (Eph. 2:9). You just came and said, "Lord, I relax; I let You live in my life." And we should *continue* as Christians in the same way. Victory in life is a gift from God: "Thanks be to God! He gives us the victory!" (1 Cor. 15:57)

When I finally grasped this concept it was such a release: I resigned as general manager of the universe and realized that the world wasn't going to fall apart! I was not only trying to solve my own problems but was taking on the international situation as well. I had the Atlas Complex: I was carrying the world around on my shoulders. But I finally got God's message: "I don't intend for you to carry that load. It's not your battle. Relax. If you're My child, I'll fight the battles."

Twice in this passage (2 Chron. 20:15, 17) God instructed Jehoshaphat not to be afraid. The king thought he had every reason in the world to be afraid—after all, it was three-to-one odds against him—but God said, "Don't be afraid." Why not? Because God promised to fight the battle.

Has God ever lost a battle? No. Never once. So you know who's going to win in the end. It's like reading the last chapter of a novel so you can know it's going to end all right, and then going back and relaxing through the story. Your problems shrink in size when you turn them over to the Lord!

Notice what else God said to Jehoshaphat: "You will not have to fight this battle. Take up your positions and *stand firm*" (2 Chron. 20:17). What does it mean to stand firm when you've got a problem, when you're facing a battle, when you're in a crisis of life? It's a mental attitude of quiet confidence that says, "I'm going to trust God."

There's something I'm slowly learning: *It is never God's will for me to run from a difficult situation.* If I do run, this will just bring back the same situation a little farther down the line. It may have a little different look to it, but it will be the same thing. Why? Because God wants to teach me that He is sufficient for any problem. If we don't learn this today, we may learn it next week. If we don't learn it next week, we may learn it next year—but eventually we'll learn it. We can save ourselves a lot of problems by standing firm and waiting on God in quiet confidence.

What are we to stand firm on? Jehoshaphat says that we are to have faith in the Lord our God, and we will be upheld; to have faith in His prophets, and we will be successful. First, we need to stand firm on the character of God. God is faithful; we can depend on Him; He will never let us down. Second, we need to stand firm on the writings that God has given through His prophets—in other words, the truth of the Bible. The Bible is God's Word, and we need to wait in quiet confidence on His written promises.

THANK GOD IN ADVANCE

The sixth principle in conquering life's battles is to *thank God in advance for giving you the victory.* The story of Jehoshaphat is fascinating because, after he consulted the people, he appointed men to sing to the Lord, to praise God for His splendor and holiness as they went out at the head of the army (v. 21).

Now get the picture. Here are these two mountains and a valley, and a big battle is going to take place in the valley. On one mountain are the three enemy nations, just waiting to devastate the Jews. On the other mountain are the Jews led by Jehoshaphat. He tells his people, "Here's God's battle plan. All of those who sing in the choir, I want you out front." So they go marching to battle with the choir in front of the army, singing praises to God.

Did God's plan work? Yes. The three enemy armies got confused and ended up killing each other! All God's people had to do was to divide up the plunder. Why did God do it this way? As a visual object lesson to teach us to praise Him in faith even before the victory.

A young boy named James Stewart was not a believer, and in fact was antichristian. His mother bought him a Bible one day, laid it on his desk, and said, "Here, Son, is your new Bible."

James replied, "What's this for?"

His mother answered, "You don't know it yet, but you're about to become a Christian."

James responded, "No I'm not. I'm going to play football and go to hell."

His mother stood up in church that night and said, "My son is about to become a Christian. He doesn't know it yet, but I'm thanking God in advance."

So James's friends began to walk up to him on the street and say, "I heard you became a Christian."

"No, it's just my crazy mother. I'm going to play football and go to hell."

But his mother told her pastor, "I want you to save twenty minutes on Saturday night for my son to give his testimony."

The Friday night before that Saturday, James was playing football when he suddenly felt God's presence right on the playing field. He got down on his knees and prayed right in front of everybody: "God, I really need You in my life. If You can make a difference, come in and change me. Save me, whatever it takes. Make me born again."

James ran off the field in his uniform, down the street, and up the stairs into his house. He hugged his mother and proclaimed, "Mom, I just became a Christian!"

She replied, "Of course! I've been telling you that for three weeks!"

This is a true story of thanking God in advance. The lesson is that *there is power in thankfulness.* Each one of us can say, "Lord, I know I've got problems, but I thank You in advance because there is no situation that You can't take care of." That's true faith—thanking God in advance.

CHAPTER EIGHT

How Can I Be Confident in a Crisis?

THE STORMS OF LIFE

The Bible teaches that there are three kinds of storms in life: storms that we bring on ourselves (as Samson and his self-induced troubles), storms that God causes (as Jesus stilling the storm on Lake Galilee), and storms that other people cause (as Paul and Silas thrown into prison). When you're the innocent party in a crisis, that last kind of storm is especially hard to take.

Storms don't play favorites; Christians have problems too. So how do we deal with these crises? How do we stay calm and maintain our confidence and courage, regardless of what happens?

God put Paul, as a prisoner, on board a ship headed for Rome. (Actually, Paul's heart's desire was to go to Rome and preach.) While on board, God told Paul to tell the crew not to leave the harbor because there was going to be a great storm in the Mediterranean Sea. But the sailors ignored what God had told them through Paul, partly because they got impatient (Acts 27:9-12).

Impatience often gets us into trouble. When we get impatient, we run right into a storm. I've talked to many crisis-ridden people who were impatient to get married, impatient to get new jobs, or impatient to move. They didn't check things out with God, and they sailed right off into storms.

Paul told the sailors, "Men, I can see that our voyage is going to be disastrous and bring great loss to the ship and cargo, and to our own lives also" (v. 10). But they sailed into the storm anyway. Why? There are three common reasons why people get themselves in a mess, whether about 2,000 years ago in the Book of Acts, or today. Human nature has not changed!

WRONG GUIDANCE FROM THE EXPERTS

The centurion, instead of listening to what Paul said, followed the advice given both by the pilot and the owner of the ship. The first reason we get ourselves into a mess is that *we listen to the wrong experts.* There are a lot of crazy ideas out in the world, and every week there's a new therapy or a new cult. Somebody will say, "The key to life is to eat bananas and yogurt."

Someone else will come along and say, "No, the key to life is to put yourself in some strange position and go ohmmmmm."

Someone else will say, "No, the key to life is to buy our seminar tapes." It seems that everybody's got a way; everybody's got an expert opinion. But the fact is that the experts are often wrong. Some people go around asking experts what they think until they find a person who agrees with them, just to substantiate their own biases. But when you start asking the wrong experts, you're going to get yourself into a mess.

WRONG GUIDANCE FROM A VOTE

Since the harbor where they were was unsuitable in winter, the majority decided that the ship should sail on, hoping to reach Phoenix and to harbor in Crete (v. 12). The second reason we get ourselves in trouble is that *we take a vote.* The fact is that the majority is often wrong. Do you remember what happened when Moses first started to lead the Children of Israel? The majority wanted to go back to Egypt, but they were wrong. We can get ourselves into a real mess by following the prevailing opinion, the most popular ideas.

WRONG GUIDANCE FROM CIRCUMSTANCES

When a gentle south wind began to blow, they thought they had obtained what they wanted, so they pulled up the anchor and sailed along the shore of Crete (v. 13). Why else do we get ourselves into trouble? Because *we rely on circumstances.* Notice that it says there was a gentle south wind. What could be better for a nice, gentle Mediterranean cruise? The sailors thought they had obtained what they wanted because the circumstances looked favorable. But it is crazy to ignore what God says, even if circumstances tend to contradict it. Things may look good right now, but you may be sailing right into a storm.

I've heard people say, "Well, this decision must be

OK because I feel so good about it." There's a well-known line that says, "How could it be wrong if it feels so right?" The fact is that feelings often lie. If God says, "Wait in the harbor," you'd better wait in the harbor, because the devil can arrange circumstances too.

As I talk with people in counseling, I hear over and over again that they thought they had obtained what they wanted but then went sailing right into a storm, even as the sailors in the Book of Acts found themselves caught in a wind of hurricane force called a northeaster. The ship became caught in the storm and could not even head into the wind.

DON'T DRIFT

When we're caught in a crisis we typically do three things—the same three things that the sailors did. Their reactions are typical for people under pressure. "The ship was caught by the storm and could not head into the wind, so we gave way to it and we were driven along" (v. 15). Later the sailors "let the ship be driven along" (v. 17). The first thing that storms tend to do in our lives is to cause us to drift. We let go of our goals. We forget where we're headed. *We forget our values and just start drifting.*

Because they didn't have compasses in those days, and because the stars were completely obscured by the storm, the sailors were really in total darkness. When you're in a dark situation in which you can't see the stars and don't have a compass, what do you do? You drift. You just let the waves beat you back and forth, and you go wherever they go. Your problems batter you back and forth. Because of these strong currents in your life you feel like saying, "What's the use? Why fight it? I'll just go with the flow."

DON'T DISCARD

"We took such a violent battering from the storm that the next day they began to throw the cargo overboard. On the third day they threw the ship's tackle overboard with their own hands" (vv. 18-19). When a crisis comes in our life, first we start drifting, and then *we start discarding things from our lives.* With the sailors it was first the cargo, then the ship's tackle, then the grain (v. 38), and finally themselves! (vv. 43-44) They jumped overboard and started swimming to shore.

The point is this: Often when we get into a crisis of life we are tempted to throw out the very things that are important to us, the values that we've hung onto in better times. We have a tendency to just throw everything out because we're under pressure and want to get rid of it all. We become impulsive. We give up on our dreams. We run out on relationships. We throw away values that we learned as children.

DON'T DESPAIR

Notice the third thing that the sailors did: "When neither sun nor stars appeared for many days and the storm continued raging, we finally gave up all hope of being saved" (v. 20). In an extreme crisis *we eventually get to the point of despair and give up all hope.* The last thing we throw out when we've got a problem is hope, and when we've thrown that away, we've had it.

The sailors were fourteen days in total darkness, in a little ship in the middle of the Mediterranean Sea, being bashed back and forth by the storm till they threw out everything and gave up all hope. Perhaps you feel like that right now. You've been going through a problem the past week or past month or past year. It's been batting you back and forth, and you've been throwing things out, and now you've come to the point of despair: "What's the use? There's no hope. This is an impossible situation." But remember the sailors: They gave up hope because they had forgotten that *God is in control.* They had forgotten that God has a plan. They had forgotten that God can inject hope into an absolutely hopeless situation.

PAUL'S REACTION

The amazing part of this story is Paul's reaction: It is a 180-degree turnabout from the way the sailors are responding to this crisis. The sailors are in despair; they say things are hopeless. They are discouraged and depressed, and have tossed everything overboard.

But Paul is calm and confident. He's got courage in the crisis. Absolutely nothing is fazing him.

The sailors' reactions were the natural responses that we tend to have in a crisis, but they don't have to be our own reactions. One test of our Christianity is how we handle a crisis. Anybody can be a Christian when things are going great, when all our prayers are being answered, when we're in good health, when our income is rising. It's easy to be a Christian at times like that.

The test of our faith is when the problems come, when we're tempted to despair, to drift and throw out the things that are really important in life. Character is *revealed* in a crisis, not *made* in a crisis. Character is made in the day-by-day, mundane, trivial things of life—the routine. Character is made there, but it is revealed when we get into a shipwreck, into a situation that threatens to swallow us up.

What should you do when things look like they're falling apart and the ship's going to fall apart and disintegrate? What should you do when you're being battered by the problems in life? Look what the sailors did: "Fearing that we would be dashed against the rocks, they dropped four anchors from the stern and prayed for daylight" (v. 29). The safest thing to do when you get in a storm is to drop your anchors. Just stand still. Situations change, and the sands of time shift. But the Bible says that he who puts his trust in God is immovable like Mount Zion (Ps. 125:1).

Often when people encounter a major problem they want to change everything else in their lives at the same time—as if they needed more change! A person will lose his or her spouse by death or divorce, and the typical reaction is, "I'm going to quit my job. I'm going to sell everything and move to a whole new location and start over." But that's exactly what they *don't* need—more change. What they need to do is put down some anchors and get some stability.

Why was Paul such a confident person? Because he was encouraged by three tremendous truths, three foundational beliefs of the Christian life, that serve as anchors of the soul. These three truths can anchor you on the rock of stability, so that when the winds of crisis blow you back and forth you will have confidence. These are truths that you can build your life on, that will stabilize you in the storm.

GOD'S PRESENCE

The first anchor in a crisis is *the presence of God*. In the midst of the storm Paul says, "Last night an angel of the God whose I am and whom I serve stood beside me" (Acts 27:23). We learn from this that storms can never hide our faces from God. We may not see Him, but He sees us. We may think He's a million miles away, but He is watching us and is with us. God sent a personal representative, an angel, to say to Paul, "I'm with you. I see you in the stormy Mediterranean Sea in that little ship."

God promises in the Scriptures, "Never will I leave you; never will I forsake you" (Heb. 13:5); "Surely I will be with you always" (Matt. 28:28); "I will ask the Father and He will give you another Comforter" (John 14:16). Over and over the Bible says that wherever we are, God is right there with us. I never go through anything all by myself because God is always with me. No matter what situation *you're* going through right now, God is with you. He is the Anchor that you can fully trust.

GOD'S PURPOSE

The second anchor in a crisis is found in Acts 27:24, where Paul quotes God's angel: "Do not be afraid, Paul. You must stand trial before Caesar, and God has graciously given you the lives of all who sail with you." God had told Paul, "I have a plan for your life. My plan is that you go to Rome. You're on board this ship because I have a purpose for your being on this ship. You're going to preach in Caesar's court; I have a purpose for your life that is greater than the temporary storm that you are in.'' The second anchor in a crisis is *God's purpose*.

Every Christian ought to have a sense of destiny. No person is really born by accident, regardless of the circumstances of his birth. You're not here on earth just to take up space; God has a specific purpose and plan for your life. Storms are simply temporary setbacks in that purpose. Absolutely nothing can change God's ultimate purpose for your life unless you choose to disobey Him. If you choose to reject His plan, He will allow you to do that, but the Scriptures teach that no outside person can change God's plan for your life. God leaves that up to you. You can either accept it or you can reject it, but no matter what happens on the outside, external forces cannot alter God's purpose for your life, as long as you say, ''God, I want to do Your will.''

The purpose of God is greater than any situation you will ever experience. God has a plan beyond the problems you're facing right now. The point is this: It's dangerous to focus more on your problems than on your purpose for living. If you do that you'll start drifting and discarding. You'll start despairing if you keep your eyes on the problem rather than on the purpose of God for your life. Then once you lose your goal you'll lose sight of the very meaning for which you exist, and you'll become purposeless.

GOD'S PROMISE

The third anchor that gives us confidence in a crisis is found in verse 25, where Paul says,''Keep up your courage, men, for I have faith in God that it will happen just as He told me.'' The third anchor is *God's promise.* Does God keep His promises? Without fail. Storms cannot hide our faces from God, because God is always with us. Storms cannot change the purpose of God, because it is ultimate. Storms cannot destroy the child of God, because God's promise is sure.

Some of you are going through devastating crises right now. Your problems are overwhelming, and you think you're going under for the last time. Let me say this from God to you: You may lose the cargo; you may lose the tackle of the ship; you may lose the ship; you may even get wet—but you're going to make it, because of the promise of God. "God said it, I believe it, and that settles it." So what do you do? Relax. Be confident in your crisis.

PRAY WHILE YOU WAIT

What should we do while we're waiting for God to fulfill His promise? The same thing that the sailors did (Acts 27:29): "Fearing that we would be dashed against the rocks, they dropped four anchors from the stern and prayed for daylight." *Anchor yourself on the truths of God and pray for daylight.*

What was the result? Morning came! When daylight came they didn't recognize the land, but they saw a bay with a sandy beach where they decided to run the ship aground. All 276 people jumped overboard and got safely to land (vv. 39-44).

In the storms of your life God says, "I'm with you." Let His truth stabilize your life and give you the confidence you need in every crisis you face. Storms cannot hide God from you. You may be going through some difficult times right now, but God has a purpose for your life. There's a reason for it all, and you're going to make it safely to land!

CHAPTER NINE

How Can I Ever Change?

What would you most like to change about yourself? If you could change one thing, what would it be? A great tragedy is a wasted life, a life that is never willing to change. Change is a necessary part of a growing life, and we need change in order to remain fresh and to keep progressing.

Most of us are interested in change. Of the fifteen recent bestsellers, ten of them were self-help books— titles such as "Thirty Days to a New You." We go to seminars and read books and try diets and listen to tapes, but somehow, the new ideas just don't seem to last. Maybe we'll change for a while, but each new idea really doesn't have a permanent effect. The main reason for this is that we work *on the exterior*, our outside behavior, instead of on our interior motives. Any lasting change must begin on the inside, and that's a work of God.

THE FOUR-STEP PROCESS

In Genesis, chapter 32, we see the process that God uses in changing us, in helping us become the kinds of persons we've always wanted to be. God wants to change us, and we want to change. We'll see how to change by looking at the life of Jacob, the father of Joseph. The incident recorded in this chapter was a turning point in Jacob's life, and serves as a dramatic example of how God can change us as individuals.

Jacob was a somewhat shifty fellow. Even his name means "cheater" or "schemer." But a turning-point experience transformed him into a new person, and he became Israel, the man whom the entire nation of Israel is named after. It was such a transforming experience that he was never the same again.

In this story we have a clear expression of the four-step process that God uses to change us into the kind of people we want to be. It's a truly encouraging message. It's a message that says we don't have to stay in the rut where we are: God will help us to change, to overcome that weakness or area in our life, if we'll just let Him.

How do we let Him? Let's look at Genesis 32:24-30: "Jacob was left alone, and a Man wrestled with him until daybreak. When the Man saw that He could not overpower him, He touched the socket of Jacob's hip so that his hip was wrenched as he wrestled with the Man. Then the Man said, 'Let Me go, for it is daybreak.' But Jacob replied, 'I will not let You go unless You bless me.' The Man asked him, 'What is your name?' 'Jacob,' he answered. Then the Man said, 'Your name will no longer be Jacob, but Israel, because you have struggled with God and with men and have overcome.' Jacob said, 'Please tell me Your name.' But He replied, 'Why do you ask My name?' Then He blessed him there. So

Jacob called the place Peniel, saying, 'It is because I saw God face to face, and yet my life was spared.'" (The word "Peniel" is a Hebrew word for "the face of God.")

What does a wrestling match with an angel several thousand years ago have to do with changing me today? There are some important insights in this incident which show clearly how God changes people. There are four steps that God uses to change us into the persons we want to become.

CRISIS

The first step is the *crisis* phase. Jacob had a long wrestling match with an angel, and the angel was really struggling, but it was a no-win situation for both of them. By daybreak Jacob was getting tired of the struggle because he saw that he could not win. It was a situation beyond his control.

The lesson we see in this is that when God wants to change us, He starts by getting our attention, by putting us in a frustrating situation that is totally beyond our control. We cannot win, and we just keep getting more and more tired. God uses experiences and problems and crises to get our attention. If we're experiencing a crisis right now, it's because God is getting ready to change us for the better. We never change until we get fed up with our current situation, with the status quo. We never change until we get uncomfortable and discontented and start feeling miserable. When we get miserable and uncomfortable and dissatisfied enough, we finally get motivated to let God do something in our lives.

A mother eagle will take the nest of her young and

stir it up. She'll make them uncomfortable and miserable, then kick them out and force them to learn to fly—for their own good in life. God does that in our lives: He makes us uncomfortable if that's what it takes, because He knows what is best and He wants us to grow. He will allow a crisis or problem or irritation or frustration in our lives to get our attention. He needs to do this because we don't change until our fear of change is exceeded by the pain we're experiencing.

COMMITMENT

The second step in being changed by God is the *commitment* phase. Look what the angel and Jacob said: "The man said, 'Let me go, for it is daybreak.' But Jacob replied, 'I will not let you go unless you bless me'" (v. 26). Jacob was committed; he was persistent; he stayed with the situation until he worked it out. He was in a situation he didn't like—it was frustrating, and it was getting him down—but he said, "I am 100 percent committed to staying with the situation until God turns it around for good."

Here's the lesson we get from this: After God gets our attention with a problem, He doesn't solve it immediately. He waits a little longer to see if we really mean business. Most people miss God's best for their lives because they give up too soon. They cop out. They get discouraged. When God allows a problem in their lives, instead of hanging in there and saying, "God, I'm not going to let go of this until You bless me, until You turn it around," they just give up and miss God's best.

Often when people come to me for counseling I'll ask, "Have you tried praying about the situation?"

They'll reply, "Oh yes, I've prayed."

"How many times?"

"Once."

We're so conditioned to having instant everything, including instant success, that if we don't have an instant answer to our one prayer, or instant success or an instant turnaround, we say, "Forget it, God." Sometimes a couple is ready to give up on their marriage just when success is right around the corner. They're ready to cop out when the solution is right there.

Even if we really want to change, we need to remember that we didn't get into our present mess overnight. Those attitudes and actions and habits and fears and weaknesses and ways of responding to our wife or husband—they took years to develop, and sometimes God has to remove them layer by layer. Usually it takes awhile for God to change you. But *don't give up*. There's hope. Hang in there. Be committed to getting God's best for your life.

Psychologists tell us that it takes us six weeks of doing something every day before it becomes a habit in our lives. Now that's why a lot of people never get into the Bible. We read the Bible for two or three days and then we miss it for a few days and then we read it for a few days. We never get past that six-week barrier and as a result we never feel comfortable with it. We've got to do it every day for at least six weeks before we start becoming comfortable with this new and good habit.

CONFESSION

The third step in being changed by God is the *confession* phase. The angel said to Jacob, "What is your name?"

And he answered, "Jacob." What was the purpose of the angel's question? It was to get Jacob to acknowledge his character by stating his name, which means "cheater" or "schemer." Jacob remembered the heartache he had caused by his scheming against his brother Esau, so when the angel asked, "What are you really like? What's your character?" Jacob admitted, "I'm a cheater. I'm a schemer." He admitted his weaknesses because he was honest. When he identified himself as "Jacob," he was admitting his character flaws.

This is an important process in God changing us, because we never change until we honestly face and admit our faults and sins and weaknesses and mistakes. God will not go to work on our problem until we first admit that we've got a problem. We need to say, "Lord, I'm in a mess. I've got a problem and I admit I made it." Then God can go to work.

Have you ever noticed how easy it is to make excuses for our problems? We become experts at blaming other people: "It's not really my fault, you know. It's the environment I was brought up in—my parents caused it." Or "The situation I'm in right now is caused by my boss at work."

Why should we confess our faults to God? To let Him know what's going on? No. When we tell God we've sinned, it's no big surprise to Him, because He knows what our problems are all along. We confess to Him because He wants us to say, "You're right, God, I've got a problem. There's my error or weakness." It's humbling to admit our mistakes, but once we do, God gives us all His resources and all His power to help us change for the better. At that point we can start becoming the persons we've always wanted to be.

This event in Jacob's life was much more than just a

wrestling match. It was an example of how God works in our own lives. First He brings a frustrating crisis, like the wrestling match, in which we really struggle with the situation. Finally we acknowledge, "It's obvious that I'm not going to win. I can't get this situation under control—in my own power I'm just going to keep on blowing it."

Then we need to continue: "But I'm going to commit myself to sticking with the situation and letting God work it out."

God replies, "I'm not going to bail you out right away, because I want to see if you really mean business. You said you wanted to change, so now I'm going to allow the problem to stay just a little longer to see if you really mean business."

If we cop out at this point we'll just get another problem of the same nature a little farther down the line. If we don't learn the lesson now, we'll have to learn it later, because God is going to teach it to us one way or the other. We can save ourselves a lot of problems by responding properly when the crisis first comes along.

COOPERATION

The fourth step in being changed by God is the *cooperation* phase. God began changing Jacob as soon as he admitted who he was and began to cooperate with God's plan. Jacob called the place "Peniel," meaning "the face of God" (v. 30). Jacob came face to face with God. Every one of us must eventually come face to face with God, and when we do that, God can change us. God said to Jacob, "Now we can get down to business. I want you to relax. Just cooperate and trust Me, and I will make the changes that you want made, and I will bless you." God didn't say, "Jacob, try real hard and use all your willpower to become perfect." That doesn't work. Willpower simply does not make permanent changes in our lives. That's attacking the *outward* circumstance. It's the *internal* motivation that makes the permanent changes, and that's what God works on.

When Jacob began to cooperate, God started working, and the first thing God did was to give him a new name, a new identity. God said, "Your name will no longer be Jacob, but Israel" (v. 28). After we have had a personal encounter with God we can no longer be the same. God changed Jacob from a cheater and schemer to an Israel, a "Prince of God." God knew Jacob's potential; He saw beneath his exterior of trying to be a worldly wise tough guy. God saw all of Jacob's weaknesses, but He also saw beneath the surface: "That's not the real you, Jacob. You're actually an Israel. You're a prince." God saw the prince in Jacob, and the former cheater began to become the man whom the entire nation of Israel was named after.

LET GOD DO IT

God always knows how to bring out the best in your life, and He knows how to do it better than you do. If you let Him, He will use whatever is necessary to accomplish this goal, because He doesn't want you to waste your life.

Do you want God's blessing on your life? Take the situation that is making you miserable right now and commit it to God. Say, "God, I'm going to commit it to

You. I'm going to hold on to You until You turn this problem around for good." Then confess the errors that you need to confess, and cooperate with God.

Notice an important point about Jacob's life: "The sun rose above him as he passed Peniel, and he was limping because of his hip" (v. 31). While they had been wrestling, the angel dislocated Jacob's hip, and as a result Jacob walked with a limp for the rest of his life. There's some significant meaning behind this, because that thigh muscle is one of the most powerful muscles in your body. When God had to get Jacob's attention, He touched him at a point of his strength. When we start thinking, "This is what I'm really good at, this is what I'm really strong at," God may have to touch that very thing to get our attention. God touched Jacob's thigh, and it became a reminder to Jacob for the rest of his life that he was no longer to trust in his own power but in the power of God. He was no longer to live in his own strength but in God's strength, and in so doing he became a much stronger person.

DON'T RUN, BUT STAND

There's another insight that we get from this incident in Jacob's life. He often got himself into trouble because he was a cheater, and he often reaped what he sowed. But every time he got himself into a mess he ran away from it. He just copped out. So God said, "I know how to take care of that temptation—I'll put a limp in his walk." Never again could Jacob run away from a difficult situation. For the rest of his life he would have to stand and face his problems, not in his own strength but in God's strength. God often puts an obvious weakness in people whom He blesses, and often the weakness is some kind of physical problem. For example, Paul had his thorn.

What about you? How would you like to be permanently changed? What's the one thing you would most like to change about your life? Maybe it's a habit. Maybe it's a weakness. Maybe it's a character difficulty. Maybe it's something that's gotten you into more trouble than you could have imagined, and now the situation is beyond your control. Maybe you're in a no-win situation that bothers and bugs you and keeps you from developing the potential that God wants you to develop.

Do you want God to change it? He will, but in His own way. He will use the processes of *crisis, commitment, confession, and cooperation.* And when He does the changing, it will be a permanent change. You won't have to worry about willpower and staying with it because you'll be cooperating with God, relaxing and trusting Him.

Maybe you've been limiting God by making excuses, blaming other people, or rationalizing. It's hard to drop your mask and say, "God, I've got a weakness. I admit I've got a problem." But until you do this, things will just stay the same as they are now.

The good news is this: Beneath all those things you know about yourself that you don't like, God sees an Israel. He sees the prince or princess in your life. He sees what you can become. He sees your potential, and He wants to change you from a Jacob to an Israel. Let God do His changing!

CHAPTER TEN

How Did I Get Myself into This Mess?

Samson was a ruler-judge of Israel for twenty years. He had everything going for him. Yet he was his own worst enemy, as he kept hurting himself. Samson had supernatural strength and good looks, and he had God working in his life, but he just blew it. He wasted his life and brought all kinds of troubles on himself.

Samson exemplifies three of the most common ways that we bring troubles on ourselves, ways that still foul up people today because human nature is universal and we all tend to fall into the same kinds of traps. Samson made a mess of his life because he made three fatal choices. If we can identify these three traps we can work out the problems that we're in right now and can avoid some problems in the future.

The whole story of Samson's life is given in Judges, chapters 13—16, but we will consider only key principles out of his life—things that got Samson into trouble, things that we can avoid.

LEARNING FROM OUR MISTAKES

First of all, *we're asking for trouble if we refuse to learn from our mistakes.* Samson had two big weaknesses in his life, and he never learned to control either of them. All of his life they plagued him, and later they caused his downfall. His first weakness was a bad temper. He often got angry; frequently he blew up. A primary motive for his actions was revenge. Samson killed thirty men to get their clothes because he burned with anger (Jud. 14:12-19). He set a field afire just to get even (15:3-5). Samson said to a group of men he didn't like, "Since you've acted like this, I won't stop until I get my revenge on you" (v. 7). Later he said, "I did to them what they did to me" (v. 11), and then he killed another thousand men.

Samson's whole life seemed filled with anger, and he never quite got control of this problem. He refused to learn from his mistakes, so he just kept committing them over and over again.

The other area that Samson had a weakness in was uncontrolled physical desire. He was physically strong but morally weak. He never really got control of this problem in his life either, and it caused his downfall. In fact, Samson's life was really a pathetic cycle of failures. He never learned; he kept making the same mistakes over and over again. For him it was really kind of a game: "How close to the fire can I get and not get burned? How close to the edge of the cliff can I get and not fall off?" Samson deliberately ignored God's principles, particularly in the area of physical desires.

Samson played this kind of game with Delilah. She kept asking the source of his strength and kept getting teased by Samson, but each time he got a little closer to the truth. As he toyed with her he was playing with temptation, and soon he got burned. But all of us tend to do the same thing. We say, "Just this one time. What's one time going to hurt, anyway? Just this one time I'm going to worry; just this one time I'm going to get depressed; just this one time I'm going to try this or that." None of us plans to be a failure—it just comes on us gradually. It's a step-by-step process, as little by little we get weakened. Our whole lives don't fall apart in one day; the problem builds up over a period of time when we refuse to learn from our mistakes.

You may be saying, "But this is an area of my life that I just have no control over. I'm defeated in it over and over again. It's a chronic area of failure in my life, and I just don't know how to overcome it. That's just the way I am."

The good news is that God says, "I will give you the power to break out of that cycle of failure." When Samson finally did that, God broke his cycle of failure and gave him victory.

CHOOSING OUR FRIENDS

The second principle we learn from Samson's life is that *we're asking for trouble if we choose the wrong friends.* Somebody has wisely said, "If you want to soar with the eagles you can't run with the turkeys." You will eventually become like the people you spend the most time with. That's why it is so important to choose your friends wisely. Samson was defeated by bad associations; he had unhealthy relationships even though God had chosen him for a special task. For even Samson's birth was a miracle. Before he was conceived his mother could not become pregnant. God told her that she would have a special son who would be a deliverer of Israel from the Philistines. So Samson was special from the very start, but his friends led him astray.

God has a special purpose for each of us, but we get ourselves into trouble when we choose the wrong friends. Here's a challenging question: Do your friends keep you from living 100 percent for God? Do they tear you down or do they build you up? Do you find yourself having to conform to things you don't like to do? The Book of Proverbs warns us over and over again about negative associations. Constant exposure to wrong attitudes and wrong values will eventually take its toll in our lives for it's always easier to pull somebody down than it is to lift him up.

What kind of friends should you have? The kind who bring out the best in you, who lift you up, who encourage you, who make you a better person.

TAKING GOD SERIOUSLY

There's another principle that we see in Samson's life, and this is really the most important one of all because we see it all through his life: *we're asking for trouble when we refuse to take God seriously.* Samson was careless about his spiritual life. He never did get really serious with God, and it showed up in more than one way.

In the first place, he was always doing his own thing. He lived for himself. His was basically a very selfish lifestyle, and he let his own personal desires dictate his actions. Samson lived by the philosophy, "If it feels good, do it." God's plan for Samson was greatness, and that's God's plan for you. He has a purpose for your life; you weren't put here on earth by accident. But

Samson's pattern was carelessness; he just kind of took things for granted and never really got serious, and the result was uselessness in his life.

Another thing we see in Samson's life is that he never prayed about anything, except before his final act, when he brought the house down. He was impulsive; he was impetuous. He did not ask God for direction. He just went ahead and did whatever he wanted to do. We would save ourselves so many problems and so much pain if we would just stop and ask God for direction before we jump into something with both feet and get all messed up. Samson turned to God only when he got in a jam. It's what you call "foxhole Christianity": "Lord, if You'll just get me out of this problem I promise I'll live for You from now on."

To a lot of people God is just kind of an afterthought, a convenience. When things get tough and tight, they turn to Him in desperation. But when everything is all right, they ignore Him.

Samson never really got serious about living for God until the very end of his life, after everything had finally fallen apart: He was captured by the enemy nation, they put his eyes out, and they made him grind grain at a mill, a job normally reserved for animals.

Notice what happened after everything fell apart: Samson finally prayed (16:28). I wonder what kind of history Samson would have had if he had prayed right from the beginning. Why did he have to wait until everything fell apart before he finally turned to God? The result of Samson's prayerlessness is that he totally lost his potential in life. He was discredited and lost his freedom; he became a slave to the people he had been sent to conquer. Samson truly reaped what he had sowed.

GOD NEVER GIVES UP

This would be a hopelessly tragic story if it just ended there—but it doesn't. The Philistines had cut off Samson's hair, which was a sign of the covenant he had made with the Lord. Samson's hair was just an outward symbol; it was not the *source* of his strength but the *sign* of his strength. When they cut his hair off, they were saying, in effect, "Samson, we're changing on the outside what's already been cut off in your heart. You're not really serious about your commitment to the Lord."

But notice that "The hair on his head began to grow again after it had been shaved" (16:22). The process of renewal began to start. Samson repented and began to pray. As he began to look to God for strength, God honored his desire. God gave him his strength back, and Samson ended his life with an inspiring act of heroism.

As you will recall, Samson was brought to the great temple of the false god Dagon so that thousands of his enemies could laugh and joke about him and also about Samson's God—the true God of Israel. Samson was placed between the two main pillars of the temple, and with every last ounce of strength that God gave him in answer to prayer, he pushed the columns aside and the roof of the huge building collapsed, killing everybody in the temple plus 3,000 people on the roof. God had sent Samson to conquer this enemy nation in the first place, and now God was able to accomplish more through Samson in his death than He did in his life. That's a sad statement on Samson's life, but he finally did defeat the enemy. Because God gave Samson a second chance, Samson had the greatest victory at the end of his life.

In a sense that is a comforting fact. Maybe you feel that you've messed up your life so badly that God will never love you and use you again—but remember Samson. God never gave up on Samson, and He has not given up on you. God sees your potential and He remembers why He made you: you were created for great things. Only as you get in the center of God's will can you discover why you were made. But if you do so, things will begin to click and fall into place. You will feel fulfilled and will become successful in God's sight as you realize that you're doing what God made you to do.

THE COMFORT OF GOD'S GRACE

There's something very encouraging about Samson: In Hebrews 11, God's Hall of Fame of people of great faith, Samson is included! Why? Because God can take a person who was a total failure in different areas of his life and still use him. If God only used people who were perfect, nothing would ever get done. But instead He uses ordinary people—those who have weaknesses and have failed in life.

What should you do if you're a Samson? Exactly what Samson finally did: turn your life over to the Lord. Give Him all the pieces, and let Him say to you, "I will give you the power to break loose out of those things that are tying you down and causing your hang-ups and preventing Me from working in your life." Only God knows the greatness and potential in your life, but you'll never bring it out on your own; He must do it in His strength. Let Him start today!

CHAPTER ELEVEN

Why Is This Happening to Me?

How should we respond when other people cause us trouble? A prime example of suffering from the troubles brought on by other people is Joseph of the Old Testament, described in Genesis, chapters 37—50.

As you recall, Joseph was the second-youngest of twelve brothers. There was a lot of sibling rivalry in the family, and the older brothers began to get especially jealous of Joseph because of their father's favoritism to him. When the problem came to a head, the brothers threw Joseph into a pit and left him there to die. But some traveling merchants came by, and the brothers said, "Let's just sell him instead of killing him." So Joseph's older brothers sold him to these foreign merchants, who took him as a slave to Egypt.

So now Joseph is in a foreign country. He doesn't know anybody, he can't speak the language at first, and he's enslaved against his will. On top of that, his master's wife decides one day to seduce him. After he refuses, she falsely accuses him of rape and he gets thrown into prison. He is lonely and hurting, and has every right to ask, "Why me?"

But notice Joseph's attitude many years later as he talks to his brothers about the whole situation: "You intended to harm me, but God intended it for good, to accomplish what is now being done, the saving of many lives" (Gen. 50:20). In other words, "You meant this for bad, but God turned it around and used it for good in my life and in your lives and in the lives of many other people."

LEARNING FROM JOSEPH

Why was Joseph able to hang in there? Because of three important truths that he recognized in his life. First, Joseph knew that *God sees everything we go through, and He cares.* That's very evident in Joseph's life. He never doubted that God saw what was going on in his life and cared about it. There's an important phrase that is found five times in the life of Joseph, each time after a major crisis or defeat: "But the Lord was with Joseph." Even when everything was going wrong, the Lord was still with Joseph.

The second thing Joseph recognized was that *God has given everybody freedom of choice.* You're not a puppet or a robot who says little prayers to God. God gave all of us freedom of choice, and when we choose to ignore what's right, God does not force His will on us. Often when we bring a problem upon ourselves, we blame God as if it were *His* fault. God gets blamed for many things that He never caused! When we see a major accident or tragedy or problem or crisis we try to sound spiritual by saying, "It must be God's will"—as if God gets enjoyment out of planning mistakes and heart-aches!

The fact of the matter is that God's will is *not* always done. God has a will for each of our lives, but He has given us free wills too. When we choose to go our own way, He chooses to limit Himself; He will allow us the freedom of choice to make mistakes and cause problems in our own lives.

He also allows other people free choices, and from their mistakes they can hurt us. In Joseph's situation his brothers willfully chose to plot against him. This was a sin, but God allowed it because He didn't make people to be puppets.

The third thing Joseph recognized was that *God is in ultimate control of the final outcome.* He can take all our mistakes, and also all the sins that other people commit against us, then turn these around and bring good out of them. Even though we may lose a battle here and there, God has already won the war. God will take even very bad things and turn them around. When we think everything is falling apart in our lives, God has the final say. He decides what is going to happen.

Consider Joseph. He was nearly killed, then sold into slavery, then accused of rape, then put into prison. His life was downhill up to that point. But God took these tragedies, turned them around, and brought much good out of them. While Joseph was in prison he made friends with the right-hand man of Pharaoh, and when this man was restored to power, Pharaoh had a dream, and this man remembered that Joseph could interpret dreams. Joseph was invited to the Pharaoh's palace and interpreted the dream: "Pharaoh, God is telling you that you are going to have seven years of good crops and then seven years of famine, so you need to prepare for this."

Pharaoh was so impressed with Joseph that he made him second-in-command over all of Egypt. Joseph went from a foreign slave in prison to the second-greatest leader in Egypt, and by so doing he saved Egypt, plus several other nations, including Israel, from starvation.

God sees what's going on, but He also has given us a free choice, and He does not intervene against our free will. He has limited Himself. But He will use even our bad choices, and the bad things that happen to us, to turn things around and bring good out of them in the final outcome—if we let Him. That's why Joseph could say at the end of his life, "You meant it for harm, but God meant it for good." The only way God could bring it for good was for Joseph to hang on, even when he didn't understand it all.

COPING WITH ADVERSITY

Perhaps you are going through a trial right now. Maybe you're an innocent party. Maybe you're the victim of a situation that you didn't cause. Well, consider Joseph's reaction. The first thing he *didn't* do was to give in to self-pity. If you're in a problem or trial right now, you cannot afford self-pity. That's one of the major causes of depression. Usually when we're in a serious problem, and our self-esteem is already at a low ebb, we start condemning ourselves and putting ourselves down, and we end up holding a pity party for ourselves.

Joseph didn't do that; he didn't blame himself. The crisis he was in was not his fault, and he tried to look at the situation realistically. When a boat is facing a storm, the way to make it is to face the wind head-on. If you let the boat turn sideways, the storm will capsize it. When storms come into our lives, the best way to overcome them is to face them head-on.

If you are in a period of discouragement because you're going through a trial, and you're asking yourself, "Why is this happening to me?" consider this: *Never make a major decision when you are depressed.* Often when we get discouraged we're tempted to say, "I'm just going to quit." "I'm going to move." "I'm going to change jobs." "I'm going to get divorced." Never make a major decision when you're depressed, because at that time you cannot exercise accurate judgment. Your focus is blurry and your perspective is distorted. Instead, face the storm head-on and don't get involved in self-pity.

There's another thing we see in Joseph's life when all those things were going wrong: he didn't give in to bitterness. After many years Joseph met his brothers again because they had to go to Egypt for grain. As they entered Joseph's presence, bowing before the second-in-command over Egypt, they failed to recognize him as their younger brother.

When he tried to tell them who he was, they were both shocked and scared. Here was a brother they had tried to kill years earlier, and now they were bowing down to him. *But Joseph forgave them.* Joseph knew that *you cannot afford the excess baggage of bitterness in your life.*

What should we do when we're tempted to be bitter? *Turn it over to the Lord.* That's what Joseph did: He maintained his faith and hope in God; he believed that things would work out well in the end, and he kept on with his spiritual life.

When things go wrong we often reject the Person we need the most—the Lord. When a problem comes into your life you may start saying, "God, why did You allow this to happen?" You may rebel against God as if it were His fault.

Instead you should say, "Lord, take this problem." God can take situations that are totally bad and turn them around. When people use situations to try to destroy you, God can use them to develop you. He loves to turn crucifixions into resurrections.

The Bible not only gives us answers to the reasons for suffering, but it also gives us practical help and comfort when we're experiencing suffering. If we will apply the following sources of strength to our life, no situation can devastate us, and no crisis can tear us apart permanently.

THE PLAN OF GOD

The first source of strength that we see in Joseph's life is *the plan of God:* "In all things God works for the good of those who love Him, who have been called according to His purpose" (Rom. 8:28). This verse does not say that everything is good; there's a lot of evil in this world, and God's will is not always done. But it says that in the life of a Christian God makes all things, even the bad things, work out for good.

God has not rejected you; He's got your best interests at heart. He'll take this situation you're going through, even if it is a terrible one, and will use it for a good overall purpose in your life. He'll bring out greater glory in the long run. God is greater than any problem you will ever face. Of course it's difficult to see how God is working in a bad situation while you're in it. But later, as you look back, your perspective is better and you can see what God was doing and how He used this situation in a great and purposeful way in your life.

When you understand this truth you can look back and say to people who give you a hard time, "You meant it for bad, but God meant it for good. You meant it to destroy me, but God used it to develop me. You meant it to tear me down, but God used it to make me a stronger and more mature person." No matter what happens—even though you lose a battle—the war has been won and the final outcome is in God's hand. He will turn failures around and bring good out of them if you give Him the opportunity.

THE PROMISES OF GOD

There's a second source of strength when we're going through a crisis: *the promises of God.* There are over 7,000 promises of God in the Bible, and we need to start claiming them. They're like blank checks; they need to be used.

I suggest that you pick out a few verses, write them down on some little cards, carry them in your pocket, and memorize them. One guy put verses on cards and stuck them on his car's sun visor. At every stoplight he'd flip the visor down and read a verse, and when the light turned green he'd flip it back up. He's memorized hundreds of verses just at spare time at stoplights, never spending any extra time. You might put some verse up on your bathroom mirror. The promises of God give us hope, and they give us strength and comfort.

The Bible says that the Scriptures were written to

encourage us and give us hope (Rom. 15:4). What we need to do is read God's promises, memorize them, and then claim them in faith.

THE PEOPLE OF GOD

There is a third source of strength that should help us when we have to go through a crisis: *the people of God* Every church ought to be a caring community of individuals where the people love each other, support each other, pray for each other, laugh together, cry together, and share their burdens together. We need each other; God meant for the church to be a strong support system as we encourage each other and help each other.

But it can't be a support system if we don't know each other. We need to get involved in some kind of small group Bible study in the church. We need to find a small group of people that we can meet with on a regular basis, and then share our lives with them and pray with them. As we do this, we'll discover that there are other people who have the same problems that we do—people who can encourage us. They will be people who have had our same or similar problems and are now on the other end; they've been through the tunnel and so they can now reach in and help pull us through.

The Bible says that God often allows us to go through intense trials and problems, and then comforts us so that we in turn may offer comfort to others who go through the same situations (2 Cor. 1:3-4). God uses us in that way; He usually works on people through other people.

THE PRESENCE OF CHRIST

There's a fourth source of strength in a crisis, and it's the greatest of all: *the presence of God in Jesus Christ—the person of Christ.* The Bible says that Jesus Christ is God's Son, that He is alive today, and that you can have a personal relationship with Him. That's what the Bible teaches, and there are literally millions of people who are living proof, who have relationships with Christ. The presence of Christ can help us through any situation. Joseph in the Old Testament was an example of what Jesus Christ did in the New Testament: the Lord Jesus suffered blamelessly for the benefit of other people. Joseph suffered so that in the long run, when the famine came to the Middle East, his policies of food storage would save thousands of people from starvation. That's a bit similar to what Jesus Christ did. Even though He was perfect and blameless, He died on the cross to save us from the terrible consequences of sin.

God has given us free wills, so He could not force His will upon us without making us puppets or robots. We live in a world where people sin and hurt each other. But when we give our lives to Christ and trust Him, He sees us through each situation and gives us the ability to see how He's going to bring it all together in the end. The cross is the ultimate example of people planning things for evil but God working them out for good and for the blessing of mankind.

Maybe you've been hurt deeply by a family member, as Joseph was—perhaps a brother, sister, parent, husband, wife, or a boyfriend, or girlfriend. If so, do what Joseph did: *Don't give in to self-pity or bitterness. Instead, take all the pieces and turn them over to Jesus Christ. Let Him bring something new and refreshing and beautiful out of that ugly situation.*

But you may be thinking, "It's just not fair. I don't deserve this." Or maybe you've got a friend who is in trouble and you say, "It's just not fair that that happened."

And I reply, "You're exactly right. There are a lot of unfair things happening in this world." And that's why one day at the end of time the Bible says God is going to settle the score. There will be a judgment day, when all of the hurt caused on innocent people will be corrected and justified. God is going to settle the score at the end of time. But for now our duty is to keep on keeping on and see what God can do in our own lives for our development instead of letting the unfair things devastate us.

So I urge you, if you're going through a situation where you're tempted to ask, "Why is this happening to me?" realize you've got a free will, God has given everybody else a free will, and God looks on and wrong hurts Him—but He has bound Himself to allow others the freedom to choose. So turn to the plan of God and see that God will turn around even an ugly situation, and use it for good if you'll let Him. Turn to the plan of God. Turn to the promises of God. Rely on them. Turn to the people of God. Get involved in a warm church where you can have your needs met and you can be used to meet the needs of other people.

But most important, turn to the presence of Christ and let Him into your life. Out of the worst, God can bring the best. That's what the message of this story is. Out of the worst, God can bring the best. Many Christians can, in their own lives, look back and say, "That is so true. Everything had fallen apart in my life and then I gave my life to Christ and He began to put it back together. Turning your life over to Jesus Christ doesn't mean that He will always take you out of the storm, but it will give you the courage and the strength to weather it. All things do not work together for good for everybody in this world. They'll only work together for good if we give God the pieces and give Him our lives, and then He works things out for good. But as long as you hold back, He doesn't work things out for your good.

So you need to believe in Christ, you need to be a Christian, what the Bible calls "born again." What does that mean? You do two things, two simple words. One word is repent and the other word is believe. What is repent? It just means to change. Change the way you think about God and your sin. It leads to turning away from darkness and turning to light, turning away from guilt to forgiveness, turning away from selfishness and turning toward God. And then, you believe. You believe that God's Son can forgive your sin, make your life better, and He wants to work in your life; that He has a plan for you and that He can take all the messes and bad situations and even your irritations and turn them around and use them for good in your life if you'll let Him. Then you'll be able to say as you look back, "They meant it for bad, when they were really sticking it to me, but God meant it for good. God used the bad things in my life. He used them to develop me and make me a better person, and I'm thankful for it."

CHAPTER TWELVE

How Can I Overcome Loneliness?

Loneliness is one of the most miserable feelings a person can have. Sometimes you may feel that nobody loves you, that nobody even cares if you exist.

You don't even have to be alone to feel lonely; you can feel lonely in a crowd. It's not the number of people around you that determines your loneliness; it's your relationship to them. In the urban world that we now live in, people have never lived closer together, and yet they have never felt farther apart.

Can you be wealthy and lonely? Ask Howard Hughes. Can you be popular and lonely? Ask Michael Jackson. Can you be beautiful and lonely? Ask the movie stars who commit suicide. Can you be married and lonely? Ask the people who marry because of loneliness and then get divorced a few years later for the same reason.

Everybody experiences loneliness at one time or another, but there are distinct causes for it and distinct cures for it. Sometimes we bring loneliness on ourselves, but at other times we're in situations that are inevitable and uncontrollable. That's the condition in which the Apostle Paul found himself as he wrote his second letter to Timothy (probably the last letter he ever wrote). Paul was a dying old man as he wrote from a prison in Rome to his good friend Timothy and urged the younger man to visit him because he was lonely.

TRANSITION

There are four basic causes of loneliness. The first cause of loneliness is *the transitions of life.* Life is full of transitions and stages. Growing older is a series of changes, and any change can produce loneliness in your life. You're lonely when you're born, and you cry until you're cuddled. The first school you went to was lonely. Getting a job is lonely. Changing jobs is lonely. Retiring is lonely. The death of a loved one is lonely.

Paul is now in the final transition of life, and he knows that his time is short—and he's lonely. He says, "I am already being poured out like a drink offering, and the time has come for my departure" (2 Tim. 4:6). He is saying, in effect, "My time is short. I know it. I may be martyred by Nero very quickly. If not, I'll die just from old age." As Paul spends his last days alone he says, "I have fought the good fight. I have finished the race. I have kept the faith. Now there is in store for me the crown of righteousness" (vv. 7-8).

The first cause of loneliness is simply the transitions of life. Any new experience that we have to deal with can be lonely. To make things worse, we tend to isolate people who are dying. Seventy percent of people in rest homes never get a visit from anybody!

SEPARATION

The second basic cause of loneliness is *separation*. When you're isolated—apart from your friends, apart from your family (because of career, or Army, or any reason)—that can cause loneliness. Paul says to Timothy, "Do your best to come to me quickly" (v. 9). Then Paul mentions his best friends, but none of them are with him, except Luke. He's in a foreign country in prison, and he says, "I miss these people." These were Paul's best friends, his previous traveling companions. Paul was a "people person"; he loved to be among people, and he never went anywhere alone. But now at the end of his life he experiences the loneliness of separation because his friends are in other countries.

Today you can just pick up a phone and call somebody. But in those days Paul couldn't just reach out and touch someone. It took a long time to get to somebody. So Paul was lonesome because he was separated from his friends.

Twice in this passage, (vv. 9, 12) he asks Timothy to "Come," and then (v. 21) he says, "Do your best to get here before winter." Why is he saying this? He's saying, "Timothy, I may not be around much longer. And I really want to see you. Come back and see me."

Whom do you need to call? Whom do you need to write a letter of appreciation to? You need to do it now, while there's still time. Help relieve someone's loneliness of separation.

OPPOSITION

The third basic cause of loneliness is *opposition*. Paul says, "Alexander the metalworker did me a great deal of harm" (v. 14). In other words, "Not only am I getting old and sitting here alone in prison, but I've been attacked." We don't know what Alexander had done to Paul. Maybe he slandered Paul's name, or attacked his reputation. Maybe he was turning people against Paul. The Greek word for "harm" in this verse literally means to oppose or resist. And to be vigorously opposed creates a truly lonely feeling.

Some of the meanest things can be said by little children on the playground. Do you remember when you were a little kid and everybody ganged up against you? All of a sudden during one recess the fickle finger of popularity turned, and everyone was against you: "You're not our friend anymore!" You felt opposed, and you felt alone. It's a lonely feeling to go through a painful experience like this, to suffer rejection while everyone else is having fun. It's a lonely feeling to be misunderstood, to be embarrassed, to be humiliated. The temptation when this happens is to draw yourself into your shell and to build up walls. But doing that only makes you lonelier.

REJECTION

The fourth basic cause of loneliness is the most serious one, the one that causes us the most pain. It's the loneliness of *rejection*. It's when you feel as though you've been betrayed, as if you've been forsaken, abandoned in your time of need by those closest to you.

Paul felt this way; he felt deserted. He says of his trial before Nero, "At my first defense no one came to my support, but everyone deserted me" (v. 16). You can almost hear the pain in Paul's voice: "When things got tough, everybody left me. When the trial got warmed up, nobody was there." Nobody spoke for his defense; everybody copped out. Rejection is one of the most difficult things for a human being to handle. That's why divorce is so painful, and that's why God hates adultery: it's a betrayal, and it hurts lives. It's an unfaithfulness, an abandoning, a forsaking, and it is a very painful experience. God says that every human being has an emotional need for acceptance, and when that need is violated, it is a serious sin.

DEALING WITH LONELINESS

There are good ways and there are self-defeating ways to deal with loneliness. One self-defeating way is to become a workaholic. You spend all your time and energy working, working, working. You get up in the morning and work all day until finally you just flop into bed exhausted at night. But eventually that takes its toll on you physically and emotionally.

Some people try materialism: They buy everything they can. "If I can just get a lot of things around me, I'll be happy." But things don't satisfy. If you were put on an island and told, "You can have anything you want except human contact," how long do you think you'd be happy? Not very long, because things don't satisfy. You can't purchase happiness. The most devastating form of punishment is solitary confinement because people need people. We need interaction. We need acceptance and love.

Some people have an affair; they look outside their marriage. Others turn to alcohol or drugs. Still others lose themselves in a fantasy world by reading novels or watching a lot of TV. Some people do nothing—they just sit around, and hold a pity party.

But Paul did four things to combat his loneliness, and they are just as approriate today as they were when Paul went through his days of loneliness. These four things are the concepts *utilize, minimize, recognize,* and *empathize.*

UTILIZE

The first way to deal with loneliness is to *utilize your time wisely.* In other words, make the best of your bad situation. Resist the temptation to do nothing. Loneliness has a tendency to paralyze you if you just sit around and do nothing. Resist that—think of a creative way to take advantage of your lack of distractions.

If life gives you a lemon, make lemonade. Whatever you can do, do it. This is what Paul did: "I sent Tychicus to Ephesus" (v. 12), and, "When you come, bring the cloak that I left with Carpus at Troas, and my scrolls, especially the parchments" (v. 13). Paul refused to sit around and mope. He didn't say, "Poor me, poor me." He didn't complain, "God, is this what I get for thirty years of ministry? Is this my reward for starting lots of churches, for being the person most responsible for the spread of Christianity in the Roman world? Is this what I get—to die in loneliness in a damp prison in Rome?"

No pity party for Paul! Instead he said, "If I'm going to be lonely I may as well be comfortable. I'm going to make the best of a bad situation. Bring my coat so at least I'll be warm."

Often lonely people don't take care of themselves. They don't eat right, they don't exercise, and they ignore their personal needs. But Paul said, "Bring my coat and my books, and I'll capitalize on this lack of interruption; I'll use it for writing and study time." This was a great change of gears for Paul, because he was an activist, a church-planter. More than anything else he wanted to be in the coliseum preaching instead of in a prison studying. But sometimes God can use loneliness for good. If Paul had been in the coliseum he would have been preaching, but God left him in prison and we got part of the New Testament instead!

Probably the only way that God could get Paul to sit still was to put him in prison. And Paul's response was, "If I can't be where the action is, I'll create action right here."

MINIMIZE

The second way to deal with loneliness is to *minimize the hurt.* Play down the loneliness. Don't exaggerate it and don't rehearse it over and over: "I'm so lonely, I'm so lonely." Don't allow the loneliness to make you bitter, and don't allow resentment to build up in your life. Paul said, "No one came to my support but . . . may it not be held against them" (v. 16).

Paul had a lot of time on his hands, but one thing he didn't have any time for was to become resentful. He knew that resentment only makes you lonelier and builds a wall around your life. It locks you in a self-imposed prison and drives people away, because nobody likes to be around a cynic, a person who's always bitter and complaining. Paul said, "I want to be a better person, not a bitter person, so I'll utilize my time and minimize my hurt."

RECOGNIZE

The third way to deal with loneliness is to *recognize God's presence*. Paul said, "The Lord stood at my side and gave me strength" (v. 17). Where is God when you're lonely? Right next to you. Jesus said, "I will not leave you as orphans" (John 14:18)—"I will not leave you comfortless" (KJV). God said, "Never will I leave you, never will I forsake you" (Heb. 13:5).

There's no place where God is not. He is everywhere at every time, and you can constantly talk with Him. As long as you understand that, you're never really alone. Prayer is a fantastic tool that you can use in lonely times. Talk to God and let Him speak to you. David learned that fellowship with God is a tremendous antidote to loneliness. He would cry out, "God, I'm so lonely. King Saul is chasing me and I'm alone in a cave. But then I turn my thoughts to You. Where can I get away from Your presence? If I go up to heaven, You're there. Anywhere on earth, You're there. I can't get away from You" (from Ps. 139). David learned that loneliness is a signal that it's time for us to become better acquainted with God.

Amy Grant's got a great song. It says, "I love a lonely day. It gives me a chance to really focus on God." So what should you do? Do what Paul did. Don't mope around; don't give in to the temptation to do nothing. Utilize your time. Make it count.

EMPATHIZE

The fourth way to deal with loneliness is to *empathize with other people's needs*. Instead of focusing inward on yourself, focus outward on other people. Instead of looking at yourself, look out to other people. Start helping other lonely people. That's what Paul did. His whole goal in life was an outgoing ministry—serving others without focusing on himself. As he said, "The Lord stood at my side and gave me strength, so that through me the message might be fully proclaimed and all the Gentiles might hear it" (2 Tim. 4:17). Paul was lonely and at the end of his life, and yet he never forgot his life's goal: to help other people.

When Corrie ten Boom was young she fell in love with a young man, and was head over heels in love with him. But he broke off the relationship and married one of her good friends. She was devastated. Nothing hurts more than rejection, having somebody else chosen over you. When she got home, her dad said something very wise to her: "Corrie, your love has been blocked and he's married somebody else. Now there are two things that you can do with a blocked love. You can dam it up inside and hold it all inside and it'll eat you up—or you can rechannel it to something or someone else, and can focus on other people's needs. You can live a life of love, meeting other people's needs." She chose to do that, as you know.

It's like the couple in agony who really want children, but can't have them. What are they going to do with that love that they would have had for their children? They can hold it in or they can rechannel it. There are lots of children in the world who need love. They can focus on the needs of others.

We need to stop building walls between us and others and start building bridges. We need to stop complaining, "God I'm so lonely," and start saying, "God, help me be a friend to somebody today. Help me build a bridge instead of building a wall."

Love is the antidote to loneliness. Instead of waiting to be loved we need to give love, and then love will be given back to us in abundant measure.

FILLING THE VACUUM

What does God have to say about your loneliness? The first thing He says is, "I understand. I really understand." The Son of God knows what it's like to be lonely. In Jesus' darkest hour, in the time just before He was crucified on the cross, as He was in the Garden of Gethsemane, all His friends fell asleep. When the soldiers came and took Him to the trial, all His disciples fled. Soon Peter denied Him three times. When Jesus took the sins of the world upon Himself on the cross He cried out, "My God, My God, why have You forsaken Me?" (Mark 15:34)

Yes, Jesus understands loneliness. So He says to you, "I understand how you feel. I care about you and I want to help you." Let Him help you conquer your loneliness as you turn to Him in prayer and reach out in love to lonely people around you!

Free Catalog of additional resources by Rick Warren

The *Encouraging* Word
Foothill Ranch, CA 92610
949/829-0300 - Fax 949/829-0400
Email: info@pastors.com
Web Site: www.pastors.com